Image Books

Doubleday

New York London Toronto

Sydney Auckland

IT'S NOT THE SAME
WITHOUT YOU

Coming Home to the
Catholic Church

MITCH FINLEY

AN IMAGE BOOK
PUBLISHED BY DOUBLEDAY
a division of Random House, Inc.

IMAGE, DOUBLEDAY, and the portrayal of a deer drinking from a stream
are trademarks of Doubleday, a division of Random House, Inc.

Book design by Dana Leigh Treglia

Library of Congress Cataloging-in-Publication Data

Finley, Mitch.
It's not the same without you: coming home to the Catholic Church/
Mitch Finley.—1st ed.
p. cm.
Includes bibliographical references.
1. Ex-church members—Catholic Church. 2. Catholic Church—Membership.
I. Title.
BX2347.8.E82 F56 2003
282—dc21
2002027481

ISBN 0-385-50568-X

PRINTED IN THE UNITED STATES OF AMERICA

March 2003
First Edition

1 3 5 7 9 10 8 6 4 2

ACKNOWLEDGMENTS

All of the stories in this book are true, although all the names have been changed to protect the anonymity of those who shared their stories with me. My sincere thanks to all those who took the time to write and send me their stories. Thanks, also, to the many dedicated Catholic newspaper editors who kindly published my letter inviting former and returned Catholics to send me their stories. And a heartfelt thanks to my agent, Tom Grady, for invaluable guidance and suggestions.

One fine February evening, over a delicious Mexican meal in Tucson, Arizona, Mike Leach, executive director of Orbis Books, and Father Andy Greeley urged me to write a book such as this one. At that time I already had considered the idea and decided not to do it. Had they not spoken in this book's favor, I might never have written it. My thanks to both for giving me the verbal nudge I needed.

I have been deeply touched by the many stories people shared with me, both those I used in the book and the many I was not able to use. To all those who "left" and "came home" to the church: It's wonderful to have you back. To those who have not returned to the church: I pray that one day you will find it possible to come home, because . . . it's not the same without you.

The Scripture quotations contained herein are from the New Revised Standard Version Bible: Catholic Edition, copyright © 1993 and 1989 by the National Council of the Churches of Christ in the U.S.A. Used by permission. All rights reserved.

For Michael Leach

and

Rev. Andrew M. Greeley

CONTENTS

PART TWO
Reaching Out to Alienated Catholics

IT'S NOT THE SAME
WITHOUT YOU

INTRODUCTION

High Expectations,

Serious Disappointments

Every time I pay our local utilities bill, I think of the mother of my best friend from high school because she works in the accounts payable department of the utilities company. I think of her because I know that even though she considers herself a Catholic, for reasons unknown to me she rarely goes near a Catholic church. As for her son, although he grew up Catholic, he has had little contact with the church in decades. He once remarked to me that he thinks of the church as "just a club, and I don't care to belong."

In that sentiment, he's like three of my other friends from high school. One had a disagreement on a point of church doctrine while attending a Catholic university more than thirty years ago, and he has been separated from the church ever since. His subsequent unhappy marriage and divorce only added to his sense of alienation, I'm sure. My other two friends simply drifted away from the church, as far as I can tell, and they feel no sense of loss.

A married couple who once belonged to the same parish as my wife and I are now more Buddhist than anything else. After they adopted two daughters they became so frustrated by what they view as the Catholic church's prejudice against women that they decided to give up on Catholicism altogether.

I know young adults who grew up in Catholic families but who feel no need themselves to be active in a Catholic parish. Some of them are Christmas-and-Easter Catholics, attending Mass only on these two days of the year. Another young adult mentions occasionally that she is a Catholic, but she seems to have mixed feelings about this and, as far as I know, rarely if ever attends Mass. A few gay acquaintances of mine appreciate having grown up Catholic but feel unwelcome in any Catholic parish.

In my own extended family, perhaps ten people are technically Catholic but they have no real ties to the church. Some of them are indifferent to Catholicism; some harbor bitter feelings about past negative experiences with a priest or nun; others married non-Catholics whose anti-Catholic prejudice keeps them away from the church for the sake of marital harmony. The children of these families have never been baptized—a source of heartache to grandparents, especially. In yet other instances, husband and wife call themselves Catholics and have their children baptized, but their participation in the life of the church is superficial and sporadic, and in a few cases their marriages are on thin ice.

In more than a few cases in my extended family, there are young adults whose parents are sincere, dedicated Catholics, but these young adults feel no connection to the church. In one case two young men from one family had unpleasant experiences in Catholic schools—to which their parents sent them at considerable financial sacrifice—and today they have no interest in being Catholic. Some young adults in my extended family cohabit with girl- or boyfriends, see nothing wrong with this choice, and have no interest in being Catholics.

Good friends of ours have been sincere Catholics all their lives. One of their sons, now a young adult, married a couple of years ago. His wife was raised Catholic, too, but she feels deep resentment about what she views as the second-class status of women in the church. The couple's wedding was in a Protestant church, but they had their recently born baby baptized in a Catholic parish.

I cite these stories from my own experience because they're so typical in our culture. The reasons for alienation from the Catholic Church are many. Parish priests or diocesan marriage tribunal personnel occasionally operate in an insensitive manner with divorced Catholics. Catholics remarried outside the church sometimes conclude that by doing this, they permanently alienate themselves from the church. Parents want their baby baptized, but they do not attend Mass regularly, and a particular priest or parish lay minister responds in a legalistic fashion, refusing to baptize the infant until the parents attend Mass every Sunday.

In some cases victims of priest pedophiles experienced distrust and rejection rather than understanding, acceptance, support, and expressions of sorrow. In some Catholic parishes gay or lesbian Catholics encounter condemnation and rejection rather than welcome and expressions of a desire for understanding.

It is not unusual for a non-Catholic spouse's religious community to seem more open and welcoming, and living in a religiously mixed marriage can seem too stressful, so the Catholic spouse decides to join his or her spouse's church or non-Christian religion. There are many stories of painful experiences associated with attending Catholic schools in decades gone by, and sometimes these experiences led to many years of alienation from the church. In some parishes engaged couples are greeted with demands for observance of regulations for marriage preparation rather than the open arms of a parish community.

Raised Catholic, as adults some conclude that because they cannot accept certain official church teachings—such as the official prohibition of artificial contraceptives or the exclusion of women from ordination to the priesthood—they no longer wish to be Catholics. The list of reasons Catholics become alienated from the church is long one. Sometimes, too, in a dominant culture that rarely supports a faith-based way of life, Catholics simply drift away out of indifference.

Not long ago I attended a novena in our parish. The term "novena" comes from the Latin for "nine," hence nine days of prayer. Part of each day's ritual included the reading of short petitionary prayers written anonymously on small pieces of paper by those attending the novena. Many of the prayers were in this vein: "In thanksgiving for my husband's successful surgery." "Please pray that I may be able to find a new job." "That my mother, who is suffering from cancer, may not lose hope."

Each and every time these prayers were read, however, they always included several praying for the return to the church of grown children, brothers and sisters, or friends. "Please pray that my daughter will come back to the church." "That my children will remember their Catholic faith." "That my husband will start attending Mass again." "Pray that God will touch the hearts of my sister and brother and bring them back to the church so they will not go on living their lives without the light of the Catholic faith to guide them." "For all of my friends who no longer practice the faith, that God will bring them back to the church."

Priests or religious educators frequently tell parents that they are not responsible if their children no longer practice the faith. In many cases the parents agree intellectually. As I write this book, all three of our sons, in their early twenties, are uncertain about their ties to Catholicism and rarely attend Mass. My wife and I agree that ultimately kids grow up and make their own choices. But like many parents, deep in our hearts we still feel that in spite of all our efforts, we may have failed to pass along to our children the most important gift of all, the one that holds everything else in life together and gives it meaning and direction—the gift of the Catholic faith. Of course, many of our friends have young-adult offspring who are in the same situation. All the same, it doesn't help that still other friends have kids the same ages as ours who wouldn't dream of not going to Mass every Sunday and whose faith really seems important to them.

Following our parish novena one evening, I heard a man say of his sister, who had been alienated from the church for many years: "She hasn't had an easy life. If only she hadn't left the church, for support she would have her Christian faith and the Mass and the other sacraments and a faith community to be with her in her struggles. I think all this would have helped her to find some direction in life. I pray every day that she will accept the grace that I know Christ offers her to come back to the church."

Sometimes it seems as if alienated Catholics are as common as can be—people who speak of themselves as "ex-Catholic," "fallen away," or "lapsed." Borrowing from the language of recovery, sometimes you hear the term "recovering Catholic."[1] Now and then you hear that people who are alienated from the Catholic church constitute the second-largest denomination in the world, after people who continue as "active Catholics." Indeed, there is some truth to this observation.

According to sociologist Father Andrew M. Greeley, most Catholics choose to remain in the church.[2] In the United States, this amounts to about 25 percent of the population, or some 60 million people.[3] At the same time, it appears that about 15 percent of those raised Catholic no longer think of themselves as such—are, in other words, alienated from the church.[4] This fact would mean that, conservatively speaking, some 9 million Americans are alienated Catholics. Other estimates put the number higher.

In fact, alienation from the church is a matter of degree. Many, perhaps most, Catholics at one time or another feel some distance between themselves and the church. Many feel estranged from the church in certain ways much of the time. But they don't feel so alienated that they pull up stakes and leave entirely. They hang in there, they plod along doing the best they can, tolerating what they find difficult to live with and doing what they can to change the church in ways they believe will overcome their alienation. In this sense, people who are estranged from the church to the point of complete nonparticipation and those who are alienated but continue to belong have much in common. Many Catholics feel some distance from the church; it's just that some of us don't let the darkness we find in the church keep us from seeing the considerable light that we find there, too.

Yes, there are things about the church that make me want to scream, or cry, or that just irritate the living daylights out of me.

One of my main sources of irritation is what strikes me as the superficial attitudes many Catholics, including some priests, seem to have toward the Mass. It bothers me when parish liturgy committees or priests make changes in the Mass that seem to be based mainly on a desire to promote a particular theological ideology. It irritates me when a priest begins Mass with remarks that seem designed to merely "warm up" the congregation, much in the style of a television talk show host. I don't like it when a priest changes the wording of Mass prayers, or adds prayers of his own, for no apparent reason except his inclination to make the prayers more "conversational" or to inject his own personal piety into the liturgy.

Another source of alienation for me is the consistent practice of giving lip service to the importance of marriage and family life while in most parishes marriages and families get no real support and are left to their own devices in a culture that erodes family relationships daily. The church's official teachings insist that the family—in its various forms—is the most basic unit of the church, but in practice the parish is the church's bottom line. In many parishes there is no real, active commitment to the support and nourishment of marriage and family life.

Along with the great majority of Catholics and the great majority of theologians, not to mention the great majority of priests, for many years I have disagreed with the church's official teaching that each and every act of sexual intercourse must remain open to the conception of a new life and that therefore the use of artificial contraceptives is unacceptable for Catholics. I think this reduces the human person to his or her physiological processes and ignores spiritual, personal, and interpersonal realities in marriage that include but transcend physiology.

At the same time, the church promotes Natural Family Planning (NFP), a method of spacing and limiting births based on abstinence during the woman's fertile times. Some couples like NFP, but many more find that it adds to rather than relieves stress in their relationship.[5]

I have yet to hear a convincing argument for not ordaining women to the priesthood. I also see no reason to not ordain married men or women. I have been offended by rude or authoritarian priests and bishops. My father-in-law tells a true story from many years ago about a pastor who took advantage of my future mother-in-law by asking her to give many volunteer hours to the parish when she had three children at home under the age of five. This so infuriated him that he came close to leaving the church.

I can remember more than a few occasions when nuns in Catholic schools were harsh, even borderline cruel to children. In the third grade I was personally embarrassed by a nun who was impatient with my apparent inability to learn long division. She insisted that I stand at the chalkboard, in front of the entire class, and try to solve a problem long after I had given up in despair, to the point that I stood there in tears. I watched the same nun hurl pieces of chalk from the front of the classroom at kids who were talking when they should not have been doing so.

When I read newspaper reports about priests who sexually abused boys, I am ashamed and embarrassed for my church. In the church I find more light than darkness, more joy than sorrow; in the church I find myself more nourished than squelched. Still, I do experience alienation; I do find darkness in the church, and sorrow, and I do sometimes feel frustrated by the church. So it's not as if Catholics in the church aren't alienated, too. We see the craziness, stupidity, and simple lack of compassion that sometimes occurs from the parish to the Vatican.

I decided to write this book for various reasons. As a Catholic who cherishes his faith and the Catholic tradition, who loves being Catholic, I would like to help as many alienated Catholics as possible to come home to the church. I know that the church isn't perfect, and I know that its leaders and other official representatives are flawed human beings who, like the rest of us, sometimes can be impatient, prejudiced, difficult to live with, insensitive, and unkind. Sometimes they, like all of us, fail miserably when it comes to acting on their faith and living out the commandment of Jesus to "love one another." Sometimes, however, church leaders give public witness to the Gospel in ways that make me proud to be a Catholic.

I believe that an adult faith includes the ability to distinguish between the church as a human institution, including its imperfect leaders and official representatives, and the living Catholic tradition, a tradition that mediates the healing and liberating presence of Christ in time and space. I believe that for all its flaws and failures, the Catholic Church, the oldest institution in the Western world, has the greatest potential of any human institution to be a source of God's unconditional love. I believe that to opt out of the Catholic community is to shoot yourself in the foot, spiritually speaking. Naturally, therefore, I would like to help alienated Catholics to come home.

If you are estranged from the church, like virtually all "practicing Catholics" I know more than a few people like you. Perhaps you grew up Catholic but no longer want anything to do with the church. I understand your reasons, and, believe me, I sympathize. At the same time, I would like to help you see that your reasons need not add up to permanent estrangement from the church—unless you choose to make them do so. It's amazing to me how often people stay away from the church for reasons that, ultimately, are buried in ancient history or old resentments that could be resolved easily.

If you are an alienated Catholic, I have no doubt that your reasons for being estranged from the church are good ones. All the same, I invite you to ask yourself if you don't lose more by staying away from the church than you gain. Without intending to, sometimes we can cultivate an outlook that says "the glass is half empty" instead of "the glass is half full." Surprising as it may sound, the church—meaning all of us who make up the church—is imperfect, and when someone who represents the church says or does something stupid or hurtful, we need to forgive the church just as we ourselves sometimes need to ask forgiveness for stupid or hurtful things we say or do. On behalf of the church, I ask your forgiveness for whatever it is that keeps you away. I invite you to come home. Let's talk about it. Chances are good that we need not remain estranged from one another. We miss you, and we would like to begin again.

I hope that this book will also offer some encouragement to anyone who would promote efforts to bring about reconciliation between alienated Catholics and the church. I want to shine a spotlight on places where such efforts are already under way and showing some success, and I want to applaud the people who originated and direct these efforts. I want to encourage reconciliation efforts to spread and grow by leaps and bounds.

My own efforts have been limited to the personal level. Unfortunately, where I live there have not yet been any organized efforts to reach out to and be reconciled with alienated Catholics. Whenever I meet someone who is estranged from the church, the first thing I do is simply try to be cordial and friendly. I try to be a listener. If the topic of Catholicism comes up—which it undoubtedly will because I'm a Catholic writer—I try to present a positive image of Catholicism. I try to show my love for the church, but I also express regrets for its failures, and I try to show that as a Catholic I can laugh at myself when it's appropriate.

I once met a young woman from another state who was visiting the city where I live. In the course of our conversation, she asked about my work, so I explained that I write books aimed mostly at a Catholic audience. She nodded politely and after a few minutes commented that she was "a very lapsed Catholic."

Since the young woman brought this up herself, I remarked, "I hope it isn't something painful that keeps you away from the church." "Oh," she replied quietly, "I'm divorced, and I wasn't married in the church, and now my boyfriend and I are living together."

"Well," I said, "one of the things I always say is that there is really nothing that should keep you away from the church. I hope you'll be able to come home sometime soon. It's not the same without you," I concluded with a grin.

"Thank you," she said, and she seemed to genuinely appreciate what I had said. I haven't spoken to this young woman since, but if and when I do, I hope there will be an opening in the conversation for me to ask about how things are going between her and the church. The point is that I tried to present a side of the church that she may not have been aware of before, a welcoming, tolerant, and forgiving spirit. One day perhaps my brief interaction with this young woman will help her to feel better about coming home to the church.

My wife, Kathy, and I belong to Saint Aloysius Parish in Spokane, Washington. One of our parish's historical distinctions is that it's the parish where Bing Crosby—recently tagged by *Village Voice* jazz critic Gary Giddins as the top popular entertainer of the twentieth century—grew up. In addition to being the site of an annual Novena of Grace attended by many hundreds of people every day for nine days to pray for the intercession of Saint Aloysius Gonzaga, Saint Al's has a close relationship with Gonzaga University. The parish sits immediately adjacent to the university campus, so it's not unusual for students to attend Mass at Saint Al's. Kathy and I always feel comfortable about inviting "lapsed" or "alienated" Catholics to come to Saint Al's because not only is it a warm and welcoming parish community, but without going to either liberal or conservative extremes there are liturgies to suit just about anyone's preferences.

It occurred to me that the fact that there are millions of alienated Catholics actually may be a backhanded compliment to the church—in some cases, at least. The truth is that Catholics tend to have high, sometimes unreasonably high, expectations of their church. Church leaders incline toward presenting the church, and by implication themselves, as God's right hand and the earthly stand-ins for Christ himself. This is powerful stuff. Regardless of how appropriate or inappropriate this view of the church and its leaders may be, historically Catholics' expectations have been shaped by this theology. One consequence is that when the church's leaders—from the most obscure parish priest or lay minister to the pope himself—fails to live up to this ideal image of the church, Catholics are sometimes so hurt and disappointed that they see no alternative but to give up on the church entirely.

In other cases, in certain historical periods, there have been widespread failures on the part of Catholic pastors and teachers to cultivate a balanced, healthy understanding of what it means to be fully human, alive, and Christian. In our part of the country, the Pacific Northwest, memories are still alive about nineteenth- and early twentieth-century Catholic missionary schools that were established on Indian reservations, schools where every attempt was made to rid Indians of their native culture and language.

Another example: During the first half of the twentieth century, prior to the Second Vatican Council in the mid-1960s, it was common for Catholics to think of sex as dangerous, primarily a source of temptation to sin. Consequently, ordinary

Catholics had considerable neurotic guilt related to sex. In Catholic schools, adolescent girls were taught to think of themselves primarily as temptations to boys, and both boys and girls learned that any form of sexual activity outside of marriage was a mortal sin. It was almost as if, for young people, the primary thrust of Catholic spirituality was a negative stance with regard to anything having to do with sex.

In his delightful novel *Good Evening Mr. & Mrs. America and All the Ships at Sea,* Catholic novelist Richard Bausch's main character is Walter Marshall. The time is the summer of 1964, and Walter is a senior in a Catholic high school. Bausch's description illustrates hilariously the experience of a great many Catholic boys during this era. Walter thinks he may enter the seminary and become a priest. He attends Mass almost every day in order to resist the magnetism of sin. "And for Walter Marshall," Richard Bausch writes, "there was really only one sin, one offense of heaven that he was always trying to fortify himself against: the sin of lust. The immense tide of impure thoughts and desires that seemed always about to engulf him."[6]

During the 1940s and '50s, especially, popular Catholicism was heavily influenced by Jansenism, a heretical form of Catholic puritanism "characterized by moral rigidity and pessimism about the human condition."[7] A Catholicism influenced by Jansenism tended toward scrupulosity and sometimes encouraged an almost magical view of the sacraments.

When a vision of what it means to be a Catholic is shaped by a stunted or distorted perspective on life and the world, it is not unusual for some alert souls to sense that this is so and bitterly reject it out of hand. The result is another source of alienation from the church, and more than a few intelligent, well-educated people became alienated because they were taught lessons about being human, being alive, and being Christian that they recognized as nonsense. They believed—understandably but incorrectly—that they had no choice but to leave the church and slam the door as they left.

As a religious tradition, Catholicism has a rich intellectual life, and many of its greatest saints were intellectuals. However, American Catholicism sometimes has come across as blatantly anti-intellectual. To earlier generations, it seemed as if Catholics were taught to never think for themselves, to simply listen to the pope and read the official church documents, do as they were told, and provide financial support to the church. The stereotypical slogan for Catholics was "Pray, pay, and obey."

Sometimes such people find the church to be less than perfect so they give up on it and go elsewhere, to another religious persuasion or philosophy or to a life of religious indifference, or they turn for meaning to a life of secular consumerism. The point is that there are numerous reasons people become estranged from the Catholic Church, and it's easy to see how this can be so. But one of the main points I want to make in this book is that in almost all cases there are alternatives to leaving the church, alternatives that allow you to remain a practicing Catholic, a member of the church that traces its origins directly back to the apostles of Christ and, through them, to Jesus himself. Reconciliation is almost always possible. I hope you will keep reading and see for yourself. If you are an alienated Catholic, believe me: It's not the same without you, we miss you, and we hope you will come home soon.

PART ONE

*Understanding the
Alienated Catholic*

"Lapsed" Catholics Are

People, Too

It is easy to think in two-dimensional terms about any group of people, including those estranged from the church. In fact, while alienated Catholics may fall into various categories—for example, those who left the church because of marriage/divorce/remarriage difficulties or because they were hurt by a priest or nun—each one is unique, with his or her own story to tell. An alienated Catholic may be angry, or disappointed, or grieving, or indifferent, or all four at various times, but each one deserves a sympathetic hearing.

Maria thinks of herself as a "nonpracticing Catholic." At thirty-four she has been married for eleven years to Mike, a man she describes as "a good husband and father" who calls himself "an atheist." Mike is definite about his dislike for religion of any kind. Maria was pregnant when she and Mike were married in a nonreligious ceremony. Because she doesn't want to irritate her husband, Maria never attends Mass and never brings up the topic of religion.

The couple's three children, girls ages eleven, nine, and seven, have never been inside a church and have not been baptized. Maria regrets this, but again she doesn't bring it up with Mike because she knows it would only make him angry. Apart from this, she says that her marriage is basically okay. "I would like for me and my girls to go to Mass," she says, "but if we did I know it would cause trouble in my marriage. So there isn't much I can do. . . ." Maria's voice trails off as she shrugs her shoulders in resignation.

Maria's story is one of the countless unique stories told by inactive Catholics. It's impossible not to sympathize with her situation, and only a fool would tell her that a solution to her dilemma would be easy to come up with. There simply are no easy answers, and the only response that seems to make sense is to tell Maria that you'll pray for her and her family that somehow the grace of God will redeem the situation. To be sure, stranger, more mysterious things have happened than for a spouse to have a change of heart.

Coming from a very different situation is Mark. Now forty and divorced, with no children, Mark was a teenager when his grandmother died. When Mark's father called a parish to ask that a priest visit and give the so-called "last rites" to Mark's grandmother, he was told that the hospital was in a different parish so he would need to call the proper parish. Mark's father called the other parish but no one answered the telephone. Calling the first parish again, whoever Mark's father talked to—Mark doesn't remember who it was—told him that there was nothing they could do. Mark's grandmother died the following morning without being visited by a priest. Mark's father was furious at "the church" and never again entered a Catholic church.

Mark took his cues from his father and doesn't remember the last time he attended Mass. Nor is he the least bit interested in doing so. "Why would I want to have anything to do with a church that would treat people that way?" he asks. Of course, Mark's life is different now from what it was when he was a teenager. His marriage ended five years ago, he works long hours, but on weekends he regularly volunteers as a Big Brother, spending time with a boy who has no father. "Working with Big Brothers does more good than all the churchgoing in the world," Mark says. "Besides," he adds, "I'm busy and I can think of more enjoyable ways to spend an hour than sitting in church. I'd rather take a walk in the park or work on my car. I believe in God, but I have no time for organized religion. Why should I let a bunch of priests dictate how I should relate to God?"

One may be tempted to argue with Mark about just how rational his father's reaction was and just how rational he is to stay away from the church based on an unpleasant experience that happened many years ago. Mark's final words may even hint at the possibility that he uses that long-ago unpleasant experience as a rationalization to justify staying away from the church when his real reason may be that he simply has never faced up to any serious spiritual or religious issues in his life. Like so many people, perhaps the real bottom line is that he is apathetic about religion.

Of course, Mark's comments about "organized religion" come

directly from the dominant secular culture, which has an un-thinking prejudice against any form of institutional religion. To reject "organized religion" is trendy today, a widely approved point of view anyone can adopt and be assured of social accep-tance with no need for any further comment or explanation.

Be all this as it may, the point is that Mark, too, is an alien-ated Catholic whose estrangement from the church has complex origins. No one should try to oversimplify his situation. In fact, chances are that whatever Mark verbalizes by way of explanation for his lack of interest in participation in the life of the Catholic Church, the actual reasons are below the level of his own aware-ness, reasons having to do with basic human fears and hopes. Per-haps those reasons will surface one day, and he will need to deal with them. For now, anyone would be unwise to dismiss Mark as just another superficial person in rebellion against God. Like Maria, Mark is a real, complex human being whom God's pow-erful love pursues at every turn and in countless gentle ways. He is anything but a two-dimensional stereotype.

Judith is yet another example of how complicated the lives of Catholics alienated from the church can be. Forty years ago, at the age of eighteen, Judith joined a community of women reli-gious. Starry-eyed, idealistic, and pious, she wanted to "become a nun" and spend her life teaching in Catholic schools. Judith had always looked up to the nuns who taught in the Catholic schools she attended, and she wanted to be "just like them."

Judith's devout Catholic parents were thrilled when she an-nounced that she wanted to "enter the convent." Her six younger brothers and sisters were impressed. Judith's friends were sur-prised when she made her big announcement, but they were proud of her, too. So off she went to become a nun.

Judith thrived in the semimonastic atmosphere during her six months as a postulant and one year as a novice. She enjoyed the regular times of daily prayer and participating in the Mass each morning, and she loved the classes she took on prayer, spirituality, and the religious life. She cherished the companionship of her fellow nuns-in-training, and she hung on every word of advice and guidance offered by the older nun who was mistress of novices. She liked wearing the traditional nun's habit. When she took her first vows, Judith was certain that this was the life for her. She looked forward with enthusiasm to her four years of college preparatory to becoming "a teaching nun."

About the time Judith completed her college education, the Second Vatican Council took place, in the mid-1960s. The upheaval that resulted in the church, and in religious orders and congregations in particular, had a tremendous personal impact on Judith, as it did on countless other men and women in religious life. Along with many other women, Judith ended up leaving the religious congregation she had joined when she was eighteen. Within a year she married a man who was a non-Catholic. Three years later her marriage ended in divorce, and Judith placed much of the blame on the formation she received as a nun. "It gave me a negative self-image," she says, "and I had serious problems when it came to sex. The Catholic Church, and religious life in particular, gave me a lot of inappropriate guilt, and to this day I have trouble trying to just relax and enjoy life. Plus, I have big problems with the church's attitudes toward women and its refusal to allow women to be priests. No thank you, very much."

Since before her marriage ended, Judith thinks of herself as "a recovering Catholic." She says that Catholicism is something she is trying to "get over." Judith reads books on Buddhism, she practices Zen meditation, and in her free time she volunteers at a Buddhist child care center. She admits, however, that sometimes she finds herself thinking about going to Mass, missing the sense of "divine presence" in the Eucharist. But she refuses to compromise her new ideals, and she thinks that maybe she could find what she wants in some other church. "I go to an Episcopalian liturgy now and then," she says, "and while I find it rather formal for my tastes, at least they don't have the hangups when it comes to women. They even have a woman bishop here."

Judith, too, is no two-dimensional stereotype of an "ex-Catholic." She is a real person with a unique history and her own particular story. Again, various easy responses to her problems may come to mind, but easy answers are not what Judith needs. A sympathetic ear and a willingness to be with her in her search would be far more beneficial.

It is important for us to get over two-dimensional stereotypes when it comes to people who are alienated from the church. But it is also important to not idealize them, either. In the case of the alienated Catholic who was sexually or otherwise abused by an official representative of the church, of course, the burden of responsibility for reconciliation lies with the church. In most cases, however, reconciliation is unlikely to occur unless the estranged person can be mature and objective enough to see some ways in which he or she may have acted in immature, selfish, or unrealistic ways that contributed to his or her alienation from the church.

Perhaps estrangement from the church is rather convenient, allowing someone, for example, to make a scapegoat of "the church." In Mark's case, yes, it was insensitive of whoever his father talked to not to be more helpful about getting a priest to visit Mark's grandmother. But for Mark this long-ago incident may be a way for him to rationalize staying away from a faith community whose tradition would challenge some of his current lifestyle choices.

In the case of Judith, her continuing alienation from the church is clearly understandable from her perspective; she has some legitimate criticisms to aim at "the church" based on her past experience. But it may also be true that "the church" is a convenient scapegoat for her. As long as "the church" is solely responsible for Judith's troubles, then she has no need to examine her own behavior and choices for ways she may have contributed to cooking up her own past troubles and present difficult issues.

People who are estranged from the church are real people with often complicated lives. Not one is a stereotype. But it's important to not idealize alienated Catholics, as if they were all wronged by "the church" and that all that is needed for reconciliation is for "the church" to apologize, admit its errors, and beg them to come back. The church isn't perfect, but neither is the alienated Catholic, or any human being. In most cases, reconciliation is a two-way street that requires an admission that regrettable mistakes were made on both sides.

Yes, someone should have found a priest to visit Mark's grandmother. But Mark is an adult now, and he should be able to see that insensitivity on the part of one person in a parish many years ago is hardly reason enough to reject an entire church and the twenty centuries of sacred tradition that hold it together.

Yes, Judith went through a formative process in becoming a nun that was unbalanced in some ways. But Judith is an adult, and she has some obligation to be objective about the past, to see why things were as they were in religious life back then. She needs to see that it's not fair of her to blame the imprudent choices she made later in life entirely on "the church." She needs to be able to look for the ways in which she is responsible for making her own bed and then lying in it.

Ideally, someone needs to help both Mark and Judith see that their complaints against "the church" imply that "the church" can and should be perfect—according to each person's ideas of perfection. At the same time, their complaints against the church imply the unspoken assertion that they themselves are without fault. The sooner Mark and Judith can see that they are not perfect, and neither is the church, the sooner fruitful conversation can begin that may lead to a reconciliation that will bring them back into a healthy membership in the Catholic Church.

It simply is not possible to produce a one-size-fits-all response to people who are estranged from the church. Because each person is unique with a unique story to tell, it is essential that each one receive a sympathetic hearing. It is also essential that each be willing to admit the possibility that he or she may not be entirely without some responsibility for being a "lapsed" or "fallen-away" Catholic. Once a two-way dialogue begins, the chances for reconciliation go way up.

CHAPTER ONE

Leaving the Church for

Understandable Reasons

Each person who is estranged from the church has a unique story to tell, and it's important to not turn fallen-away Catholics into mere stereotypes. Still, it is possible to identify the most common reasons people become estranged from the church. In this chapter we will look at these reasons and listen to the stories of a few people who fit into each group.

MARRIAGE, DIVORCE, AND
REMARRIAGE ISSUES

One of the most common reasons people become estranged from the church is directly related to experiences of marriage, divorce, and remarriage. The divorce rate among Catholics is virtually identical to that of the general population, yet people continue to think that being Catholic and being divorced are completely incompatible. While the church's teaching on the permanence of marriage has not changed, today in most dioceses there is greater understanding of the reasons that marriages fail. Consequently—again, in most dioceses—a more compassionate policy is in effect with regard to the granting of annulments.

A church annulment is simply a decree that, in retrospect, evidently a sacramental marriage never existed due to the presence of some impediment. This impediment may have been the inability of one or both partners to give full and real consent due to immaturity or a psychological condition, for example; or there may have been a failure on the part of the couple—or the priest—to observe the proper form or procedure for being married in the church.

An annulment does not say that the marriage was illegal or that any children born to the couple are illegitimate, or anything like that. An annulment says nothing about the children at all. It is purely an acknowledgment that the marriage never actually existed from the beginning, as far as the church is concerned, due to some impediment. Once the nullity of the marriage is established by the annulment procedure, both parties are free to remarry in the church.

In most cases, once a civil divorce is finalized, it is possible for a couple married in the church to obtain a church annulment in order to remarry. Nevertheless, misinformation concerning the church's policies with regard to divorce and remarriage continues to circulate. The following true stories illustrate the reasons related to marriage, divorce, and remarriage that people become estranged from the church. In fact, we could view each of these as a subcategory, since people become alienated from the church for reasons related to each one.

Linda and Bill

Years ago Linda and Bill decided to marry. Linda was a committed, practicing Catholic and a teacher in a Catholic elementary school. Bill was raised Catholic but stopped attending Mass during his teenage years and became indifferent about religion. He respected Linda's feelings about going to Mass on Sundays, however, and promised her that he would never object to her involvement with the church. He also assured her that he would put no obstacles in the way of their children being baptized and raised as Catholics.

When Linda and Bill approached a priest at her parish to plan their wedding, however, he gave the couple a stern lecture, to Bill about being "in a state of mortal sin" and the need for him to return to the church; to Linda about what a big mistake it would be to marry a "fallen-away" Catholic. The priest dismissed the couple, telling them to resolve their religious issues and then come back again.

Bill was furious. Linda felt hurt, disappointed, and angry. After some thought, she declared that she wanted nothing more to do with a church that would treat them in so insensitive a manner. Linda finished out the year teaching in the Catholic school, then found a teaching position in a public school. The couple explained to their respective parents what had happened, and a few months later they were married in a Protestant church. Following their wedding, however, they became nonchurchgoers, and none of their four children was baptized or raised with any religious instruction.

In retrospect, it may seem easy to condemn the priest Bill and Linda met with for pastoral insensitivity and for having a legalistic faith. Who knows for sure what the priest was thinking or whether his intentions were good? Still, the reasons Bill and Linda became estranged from the church are understandable. At a particularly sensitive moment in their life together, an official representative of the church responded to the couple with a legalistic, judgmental lecture.

Although the unfortunate experience of Bill and Linda happened many years ago, they are still bitter about it. They remain separated from the church to this day.

Bonnie and Frank

When Bonnie and Frank met and fell in love in the early 1970s, Frank was Catholic and Bonnie had been raised in a Presbyterian family. Both had been active in their respective church's youth activities, and after they met as students at a state university and their relationship grew serious, they talked about their religious convictions. Each understood that the other would never want to change religions. After they married, however, living with two churches became too much for Bonnie.

Frank never pressured her one way or the other, but finally Bonnie decided to attend an inquiry class at Frank's Catholic parish. With some reading and discussion behind her, particularly on the history of the church, Bonnie converted to Catholicism. "It seemed to me that historically you would have to say that the Catholic Church was the one church founded by Christ," Bonnie explained. Her parents and siblings were sad and disappointed, but Bonnie felt that her choice was the best one for her own marriage and her own future.

Fifteen years into the marriage, however, Bonnie and Frank's relationship was constantly in conflict. The couple had been unable to have children, and neither was willing to adopt. Bonnie accused Frank of spending too much time working and of drinking too much. Frank complained that Bonnie was irresponsible with the couple's finances. As the quality of their marriage deteriorated, the couple attended Sunday Mass sporadically. One day Frank announced that he wanted a divorce. Bonnie wasn't surprised, and she agreed. The couple separated, and their divorce was final six months later. Bonnie remained a practicing Catholic.

After the divorce, Frank's alcohol consumption became so problematic that his employer began to notice. Frank's story mirrored that of countless alcoholics down through the decades. Then one rainy summer morning Frank woke up lying behind a tree in a city park with no memory of the previous twenty-four hours. He realized this was it. He had to get some help. To make a long, sad story shorter, with the help of Alcoholics Anonymous Frank got his life back together. After a couple of years of sobriety, he began to think about patching up his relationship with the church, too. But Frank thought that his divorce would be an obstacle to receiving the sacraments, so for twenty-two years he stayed away.

Frank was mistaken about this, of course, and eventually he realized his mistake. Divorce by itself is no reason to remain alienated from the church. Still, more than a few divorced Catholics live with this mistaken assumption.

Tonia and Robert

Even more frequently, however, remarriage following a divorce becomes an alienating issue for Catholics. Tonia was married for twenty-three years, and after her divorce she continued to attend Mass. However, she began to feel uncomfortable in the parish she and her ex-husband had belonged to. Friends there expressed sympathy, and no one was outright rude to her about being divorced, but she didn't feel at home there anymore. Fortunately, Tonia lived in a larger city so she became a member of another parish where she could "blend in" more or less anonymously, which she said was what she needed at that point in her life.

A couple of years later Tonia met Robert, whose wife had died a few years before. Tonia and Robert began dating, and within a few months they both knew that their relationship was more than casual. They began to discuss marriage, but they realized that Tonia would need to obtain a church annulment of her first marriage before they could be married in the church, which they both wanted to do, even though Robert was not a Catholic. Tonia contacted the diocesan marriage tribunal office, and the person she talked to explained that it could take up to a year or more to complete the annulment process.

Tonia and Robert agreed that they should wait until Tonia's annulment was in hand before they married. A couple of weeks later, however, Tonia received a call from the marriage tribunal informing her that they were having trouble locating her ex-husband from whom, ideally, they would like to obtain written testimony. Tonia was surprised because she had no idea her ex-husband had moved. She contacted one of her grown children, however, and he gave Tonia the new address and phone number in another city. Tonia called the marriage tribunal and gave them the information.

Three weeks later another call from the tribunal informed Tonia that her ex-husband refused to cooperate with the annulment process. This was not an insurmountable obstacle, but it would slow things down. Also, with the backlog of annulments the tribunal was dealing with, it could now take as long as two or three years before an annulment could be completed. Both Tonia and Robert were discouraged by this news. Robert suggested that they could be married in a civil ceremony, then when

Tonia's annulment did come through they could have a church wedding. Tonia was reluctant to do this, but she finally agreed, even though she knew that according to church rules if she remarried outside the church she could no longer receive the sacraments until her annulment was finalized.

Tonia wasn't angry about the church's rules in this regard, but she decided that if she couldn't receive Communion she would rather stay away from the church entirely. So after she and Robert were married she stopped attending Mass and waited for her annulment. During this time Tonia felt alienated from the church, and the more she thought about it, the more she thought that the church's legalistic mentality was responsible for her alienation. Why couldn't the church be more understanding of and compassionate to people in her situation? Tonia finally went to talk with a priest at the parish where she had been attending Mass on Sundays. The priest explained the theological reasons, but Tonia left without being satisfied with his answers, and she became more and more bitter.

Finally Tonia decided she wanted nothing more to do with a church that would treat people like her in such an insensitive manner. When, about eighteen months later, the annulment process was completed, Tonia refused to sign the papers. All this was some ten years ago.

BEING HURT OR OFFENDED
BY A PRIEST OR NUN

The number of alienated Catholics who left the church because they were hurt or offended by a priest or nun is not insignificant, particularly among Catholics who grew up prior to the mid-1960s' Second Vatican Council. Stories of harsh nuns in Catholic schools and orphanages have taken on the characteristics of cultural mythology. Of course, incidents widely reported in the media of boys abused by priest pedophiles have done significant damage to the image of the Catholic priesthood.

The following true stories are similar to many reported by people who are alienated from the church. Each one illustrates the tremendous impact a single individual in a key church-related position can have on another person's life. Regardless of whether a person is justified in abandoning the church because of the behavior of one priest or because of the cruelty of one nun, the fact is that this happens. Sometimes the stories people tell have so much in common—the insensitive, legalistic priest stories, the mean Catholic school nun stories—that they become virtual stereotypes. Lest stereotypes be taken for reality, however, it is important to have some true, specific accounts from those with legitimate complaints.

Joe

Joe is in his mid-sixties now, but fresh in his memory are the years he attended Catholic elementary and high schools in the 1950s. Countless Catholics have fond memories of their years in Catholic schools, but there are also some like Joe whose experience left them wanting nothing to do with being Catholic. Joe's memories are of strict nuns who punished classroom misbehavior by giving an open-hand stinging whack with a ruler. Joe recalls that when he was in the fourth grade he forgot one of the Latin prayers he was supposed to recite as an altar server. After Mass, the priest gave Joe a tongue-lashing that left him in tears. Later, in a high school staffed by religious brothers, Joe recalls lectures that, he says, left him with heavy guilt feelings regarding anything related to sex.

After he graduated from high school, Joe joined the Army. He wasn't getting along very well with his parents at the time, and their pleas that he go to Mass only added to his determination to stay away from anything having to do with the church. The only times Joe has been near a Catholic parish in all these years is for weddings and funerals. His own wedding was a civil ceremony conducted by a justice of the peace, and he and his wife raised their four, now grown, children with no religious instruction. Joe continues to attribute an adult lifetime away from the church to unhappy experiences in Catholic schools.

Anna

Looking back, Anna describes herself during high school as wild, rebellious, and constantly at odds with her parents. When, at age eighteen, she left home for good, Anna says she also left the church for good. She believes now that leaving the church was inseparable from leaving home because the Catholic faith was so important to her parents that she could hardly leave one without leaving the other.

Some years later Anna married—outside the church, of course—and a few years after that her first child was born, a daughter. She found herself thinking that she wanted to have her child baptized, but she had no intention of becoming a practicing Catholic again herself. As Anna tells the story, she drove with her infant daughter to the nearest Catholic parish, went to the parish office, and asked about having her baby baptized. The priest Anna talked with asked if she was a member of the parish, and, of course, Anna had to say no. He then asked if she was a practicing Catholic, and she said no again. The priest told Anna that he couldn't baptize the baby of a "fallen-away" Catholic. That was the extent of the conversation.

Angry and tearful, Anna left the priest's office. She decided that if that was how the church treats people like her, she didn't want to have her baby baptized after all. She couldn't believe that the priest could be so rude. Anna's daughter, and her other two children, are all teenagers now, and none of them was baptized.

Martin

In the early 1960s, Martin attended a high school seminary. He admired the priests in his parish while he was in grade school, and he enjoyed being an altar server. His parents were surprised that Martin wanted to attend the diocesan minor (high school level) seminary near a town two hours' drive from his home, but they were proud of him for making this choice. As good Catholics, they were pleased that one of their sons would even think about becoming a priest.

During his second year in the minor seminary, which was a boarding school, one of the priests on the faculty began inviting Martin to go for walks after the evening meal two or three times a week. The priest said that the purpose of these walks was to counsel Martin about his vocation to the priesthood. One evening the priest asked Martin to come to his room in the faculty residence. This was the beginning of a pattern of sexual abuse that lasted for about two months, with the priest warning Martin that if he told anyone, he would be expelled.

After two months, the priest no longer invited Martin to go for after-dinner walks, and the pattern of sexual abuse ended. Martin simply refused to think about what had happened and repressed his memories of the abuse. He never totally forgot what had happened, but from then on he refused to think about it. If memories ever came to him, he would immediately push them aside and think about something else or do something to get the memories out of his mind. Within six months, Martin hardly ever thought about what had happened, and a year after the last incident he had all but totally repressed his memory of being sexually abused.

Following graduation from the minor seminary, Martin decided that he would not go on to the college-level seminary. Instead, he would attend a state university and perhaps think about returning to the seminary after he earned his degree. By the time he finished college, Martin no longer had any interest in becoming a priest. He rarely attended Mass and for all practical purposes thought of himself as a "fallen-away" Catholic. He decided to work for a graduate degree in psychology. Later, he thought, he might enroll in medical school and go on to become a psychiatrist.

In the course of his graduate studies, Martin learned how sometimes people repress unpleasant memories, and he began to recall what had happened to him during high school. The more he remembered, and the better he understood the abuse he had been subjected to, the more upset and angry he became. Martin consulted an attorney about what steps he could take to seek compensation and ended up taking legal action against the diocese that operated the minor seminary—now closed—and against the priest who had abused him, who was now the pastor of a city parish. The priest denied the charges, the diocese supported the priest, and the legal action became headline material in newspapers and on television news programs.

By the time the legal action came to an end, eighteen months later, Martin was even more bitter and angry than he had been before. The diocese agreed to an undisclosed cash settlement out of court, and Martin declared publicly that he had nothing but contempt for the Catholic Church.

DISAGREEING WITH OFFICIAL CHURCH
TEACHINGS OR TRADITIONS

People sometimes leave the church because they cannot agree with official church teachings, doctrines, or traditions. Usually these are not teachings central to Christianity. Most common among these today are the church's official prohibition against the use of artificial contraceptives, its declaration that the church cannot ordain women to the priesthood, and the church tradition that requires that all priests be celibate. (There are rare exceptions to the celibacy rule, such as the ordination of a married former Protestant minister to the priesthood.)

George and Clara

Back in the 1960s George and Clara were active in the Christian Family Movement (CFM), a Catholic organization designed to support marriage and family life and help people to grow in their faith. For a few years the couple watched eagerly as the lead CFM couple participated on a papal commission established to study the issue of birth control and to advise the pope on whether he should change the traditional Catholic prohibition of artificial contraceptives.

Along with a great many other CFM couples, George and Clara wrote long letters explaining their experience as a Catholic married couple, letters that went to the lead CFM couple, to help them in their work on the papal commission. In their letters George and Clara told stories of their own struggle with the issue of birth control, their experience of the failure of the "rhythm method," and their ultimate conviction that artificial contraceptives could be used for unselfish reasons. Like the great majority of CFM couples, they declared that in their opinion, for the good of marriages and the spiritual well-being of Catholic couples, the church prohibition should be changed to allow for the use of artificial contraceptives. Most members of the papal advisory commission ultimately agreed and advised the pope to change the church's position on birth control.

In June 1968, Pope Paul VI issued the encyclical *Humanae*

Vitae, in which he reiterated the church's traditional prohibition of artificial contraceptives. George and Clara were devastated. They couldn't believe that the pope would turn a deaf ear to his own advisory commission and to the witness of so many Catholic married couples, theologians, and other experts. Eventually George and Clara decided that they could no longer belong to a church that would cling to a teaching that was so obviously in error.

George and Clara have been away from the church since 1969. Their five children are grown with families of their own, and none of them is a practicing Catholic. They have not joined another church. Along the way they also found themselves in disagreement with other church teachings, but they identify *Humanae Vitae* as the main cause of their estrangement from the church.[1]

Today the overwhelming majority of Catholic married couples see no need to choose between remaining in the church and using artificial contraceptives. Most use contraceptives and continue to practice their faith in good conscience. So the decision George and Clara made to leave the church over this issue back in 1969 may seem like an overreaction. Today's younger couples find it difficult to imagine a church whose dictates people would obey in what may seem like a blind and unthinking manner. But this overlooks the way most Catholics understood faith prior to the papal birth control encyclical.

In those days, to be "a good Catholic" meant you followed the rules, period. Otherwise, you weren't "a good Catholic," and you were kidding yourself about being a Catholic at all. It was primarily due to *Humanae Vitae* that most Catholics eventually came to understand that when push comes to shove, even according to the most traditional Catholic point of view, and after making a good-faith effort to become fully informed on the issue at hand, you must follow your own conscience. Conservative

Catholics, on the other hand, tend to see no possibility of having an "informed conscience" that disagrees with the official church teaching.

Most Catholics today take for granted the need to form and follow your own conscience. Prior to the birth control encyclical, this simply was not the case. George and Clara made what they thought was the only choice they could make, either to follow the rules or to leave. For them it had to be a choice between conscience and church, and they chose the former. While today this seems like a false conflict, it makes sense when viewed in the historical context in which they made their choice. That George and Clara continue to abide by the decision they made in 1969 reflects the fact that, even today, they have a strictly conservative understanding of what it means to belong to the Catholic Church.

Susan

Susan is fifty years old and has been married for twenty-six years. She grew up in a large Catholic family and attended Catholic schools from grade school through college. Although she wouldn't describe herself as a feminist, Susan believes in women's equality. In college she read the writings of contemporary secular feminists such as Betty Friedan and Gloria Steinem, and since then she has read books by Catholic feminists such as Sister Joan Chittister, O.S.B., and Elizabeth Schussler Fiorenza. During college she stopped attending Mass because she objected to the church's refusal to ordain women to the priesthood.

Two years after she graduated from college, Susan met and married Edward, a young man who also had been raised Catholic but whose participation in the life of the church had been irregular since he finished college. Attending graduate school, he gradually became what he terms "a nonpracticing Catholic." Susan and Edward eventually decided to live together, then two years later they were married. Edward understood Susan's disagreement with the Catholic church's tradition of not ordaining women, and the couple's wedding was in an Episcopal church.

Three years later Susan and Edward's first child, a boy, was born, and they agreed to have him baptized in a Catholic parish. But they continued to go to the Episcopal church on Sundays. Neither is pleased with the worship experience they have in this church, but Susan in particular is adamant about having nothing to do with the Catholic church as long as the official teaching of the church rules out the ordination of women to the priesthood. Susan believes that this leaves all women in a second-class status in the church.

NO LONGER BELIEVING IN
ORGANIZED RELIGION

Steve

If anyone asks Steve about his religious beliefs, he says that he was raised Catholic but outgrew the church as an adult. The forty-year-old divorced father of three sometimes he refers to himself as "a recovering Catholic." Steve is one of the many people today who declare that they believe in God but have no use for organized religion. Explaining, Steve says that he doesn't see why a religious institution should get between him and God. He sees no reason for churches, priests, and religious doctrines. On a sun visor in his car Steve has a badge that reads "My karma ran over my dogma."

Drawing from various sources, Steve put together what

he refers to as his "spirituality." Steve uses whatever he finds attractive and helpful to support this spirituality. He reads widely about various Eastern religions and says that he particularly finds Zen meditation helpful. He sometimes burns incense and strikes a little gong as part of his meditation practice. Steve takes an interest in the various health-related issues he reads about in New Age books and magazines, and about two years ago he became a vegetarian. He adds that he does not believe that an "organized religion" can possibly fill the spiritual needs of unique individuals. Catholicism, he says, is the most organized religion of all, and he thinks that it maintains its "power over people" by inculcating guilt. Steve says that he doesn't need "all that Catholic guilt." He prefers a life based on "being in harmony with the cosmos."

NOT BELIEVING IN GOD ANYMORE

Sarah

Sarah, age twenty-eight and single, grew up in a large Catholic family and says she sometimes thinks back fondly on her childhood. But she insists that her parents, without realizing it, sold her "a bill of goods." She believes that all religions are based on the illusion that there is a God, "a big fatherly Supreme Being in the sky." She also believes that the Catholic Church keeps people "hemmed in with all its laws and regulations" and restricts human freedom. Sarah calls herself "a humanist atheist," which means that she does not believe there is a God, but she does believe that all of life must take the good of human beings as its ultimate purpose.

Sarah thinks that Catholicism is "a fairy tale of sorts." She doubts that the Gospels are historical, and she thinks that Jesus was just a good man whose followers, after his death, "inflated him into a man-god." When Jesus died on the cross, Sarah says, that was it. "He was as dead as a doornail, and he stayed dead, and all the rest is a fairy tale."

The one aspect of the Catholic Church that Sarah continues to admire is its charitable works. She praises the work of Catholic agencies that help the poor both in the United States and in other countries. She also admires Catholic nuns and priests who serve the poor and oppressed in Third World nations. But she believes that their motivation is based on an illusory belief in God and Jesus. She thinks those who serve the poor should be able to do so based on humanistic ideals and goals alone.

THINKING THE CHURCH IS
IRRELEVANT OR BORING

John

At age twenty-five, John is unmarried and works long hours as a sales representative for a pharmaceuticals company. Although he grew up in a Catholic family, he stopped attending Mass during high school and has had no interest in the church since then. He says that he sees no reason to go to church because "the whole thing seems boring" to him. John remarks that the church looks to him like nothing more than a big club, "and I have no interest in being a member."

John doesn't see what the point is of being Catholic or being involved in the church. He has no firm conviction one way or the other about God and says that he supposes that he could be called an agnostic. "I don't know one way or the other, and I'm not really interested in the question; the whole thing seems irrelevant to my life and the real world."

Two years ago John began dating a young woman, and it turned out that she was an active Catholic. As the relationship progressed, it became clear that being Catholic was important to the young woman, and when she realized that John found the church "boring" and was not willing to reconsider, the relationship ended. John says that he is still "irritated" by this, and in some way he blames the church for coming between him and a young woman of whom he was genuinely fond. "The whole religion thing is such a drag, if you ask me," he concludes.

DISAPPOINTMENT WITH THE CHURCH FOR BEING TOO PROGRESSIVE OR NOT PROGRESSIVE ENOUGH

G. K. Chesterton, the frequently quoted early twentieth-century English convert to Catholicism, once said: "Catholics know the two or three transcendental truths on which they do agree; and take rather a pleasure in disagreeing on all the rest."

There is considerable truth to Chesterton's wry wit regardless of the era. Since the Second Vatican Council, however, the disagreements have been especially noticeable and the divisions between liberals and conservatives particularly pronounced. Today's serious disagreements tend to be more ideologically based than issue driven. Catholics on the extreme right and extreme left tend to be ideologically motivated rather than merely having a specific issue or two about which they disagree. The differences are based on a whole theological vision of the church, or theological ideology, according to which all issues are judged.

Especially on the very conservative side, actual divisions have occurred on the part of groups wanting to preserve the traditions, customs, and practices of the pre–Vatican II church. This divisiveness led to the establishment of sects that try to duplicate the pre–Vatican II church in as many ways as possible. The conservatism of other former Catholics is more individualistic and leads them to abandon any semblance of Catholicism and align themselves with doctrinally conservative, biblically fundamentalist, evangelical Christian churches or sects.

On the extreme liberal side, estrangement from the church most often takes the form of separation without the establishment of alternative church communities. Those on the far left who become estranged from the church tend to remain isolated from the church as individuals, or else they join other already existing liberal churches, move to an Eastern religion such as Buddhism, or to a New Age sect, or become active in a secular group such as the Sierra Club.

The vast majority of Catholics fall someplace in the middle of the conservative/liberal spectrum, and they continue to participate, to one degree or another, in the life of the contemporary Catholic Church. But it's not difficult to find ordinary Catholics who became alienated from the church over issues related to the post–Vatican II renewal. Conservative alienated Catholics most often complain that the liturgical renewal launched by Vatican II ruined the Mass by taking away its sense of mystery and transcendence. Liberal alienated Catholics charge that the renewal begun following Vatican II was abandoned and the church is stagnant today. Specific issues most likely to lead liberal Catholics to estrangement from the church include the official Catholic exclusion of women from the ordained priesthood, and—especially for an older generation—the church's official prohibition of artificial contraceptives.

Bill and Teresa

Now in their mid-sixties, Bill and Teresa have been married for thirty-five years. Both grew up Catholic, attended Catholic schools, and sent their five children to Catholic schools. During the 1970s the couple grew increasingly dissatisfied with the effects on the church of the post–Vatican II renewal. They found the new Mass "pedestrian" and the music frequently "silly." They missed the old Latin Mass, and it seemed to them that the church was going out of its way not just to adapt to the times but to model itself after whatever trends were fashionable. Nuns no longer lived in convents and taught in Catholic schools, and priests went around in ordinary clothing, and some insisted that people not call them "Father." It seemed to Bill and Teresa that marriage was no longer sacred, so easily was the church handing out annulments left and right.

The final straw came, Bill said, when the pastor of their parish announced at Mass one Sunday that he had decided to leave the priesthood to marry. Bill and Teresa were scandalized; they couldn't believe their ears. During the following week the couple came to the conclusion that the church had lost its true identity and was no longer the true Catholic Church. They would need to search for the true church wherever they could find it.

About this time, Bill and Teresa heard of a traditionalist Catholic group in a nearby city. They went to the church used by this group, and there they found the Mass being said in the old way, in Latin. There were priests acting like priests were supposed to act, and nearby was a convent filled with young nuns wearing the old-style habits, nuns who taught in the school next door to the church. Talking with the priest after Mass, Bill and Teresa were impressed with his explanation of who this group was and why the current pope was not a true pope.

Returning home, Bill and Teresa read the literature the priest gave them and decided that the true Catholic Church existed not in their old parish but in this group. They decided to join, and within six months they sold their house and moved to the city where the traditionalist group was so they could be nearby and attend Mass each morning. Now, more than twenty years later, they are pleased with their decision, and they have helped other people to make the transition from what they call the "false" Catholic Church to the "true" Catholic Church of which they are members.

Bill and Teresa admit that now and then they wonder about the Catholic Church they once belonged to and the fact that, "unfaithful as it is," it still has St. Peter's Basilica in Rome, which they call "the most ancient symbol of the true church." They wonder if their church will ever be able to get the old, "unfaithful church" to "return to the truth." They don't think about this often, however. Bill and Teresa are content to stay with their church because it retains the "ancient Catholic truth."

Carl

During the years right after the Second Vatican Council, Carl was a young adult and recent graduate from a prominent Catholic university. He grew up in a heavily Catholic neighborhood in the Midwest, began serving as what was called in those days an "altar boy," and during his eighth-grade year seriously thought about going to the minor seminary for high school.

The Jesuits who taught at the college prep high school Carl attended offered a rigorous intellectual formation according to the pre–Vatican II model of Jesuit education. Carl left high school knowing why he was a Catholic and understanding the reasons for the superiority of the Catholic faith to all other religions and philosophies. The required philosophy and theology courses Carl took in college added to his store of knowledge and deepened his Catholic convictions.

When the Second Vatican Council sparked a tidal wave of changes in the church, Carl was thrilled and optimistic about the future of the church. During the Vietnam War, in the late 1960s and early '70s, Carl participated in antiwar activities. He was enthusiastic about the changes in the church, especially having the Mass in English and the new music being used that utilized guitars and other instruments instead of organ music. Carl loved to attend "folk Masses" where songs by an ex-seminarian named Ray Repp were popular.

Carl married in 1970, and he and his new wife participated in public discussions organized by a young priest on topics from "the new Catholic laity" to marriage and birth control. In the wake of *Humanae Vitae,* Pope Paul VI's encyclical that reaffirmed the church's traditional condemnation of artificial methods of birth control, Carl and his wife wrote letters to both secular and Catholic newspapers expressing outrage. As the year passed, however, Carl gradually became disillusioned with the progress of the church renewal. Also, after ten years of marriage and no children, Carl and his wife divorced.

Carl continued to attend Mass, but by the mid-1980s he began to drift away from the church, taking part more and more regularly in worship services at a Unitarian church. He was impressed with the "intellectual honesty," "appreciation for the arts," and "respect for individual points of view" that he found there. Carl has no time for "nonsense like dogmas and doctrines, and the Catholic opposition to birth control is just plain silly." By the end of the 1980s Carl was calling himself an ex-Catholic who was now a Unitarian. Today Carl is completely disinterested in the Catholic Church.

Charles and Linda

When Charles and Linda married in the early 1970s, he was a Lutheran and she was a Catholic. Prior to the birth of their first child, they took turns attending each other's churches. After their daughter was born, however, Charles agreed to become a Catholic so they would have one family religion, and their daughter was baptized a Catholic. They attended Mass each Sunday at their local suburban Catholic parish, a moderate to liberal parish of some one thousand households. After a few years, Charles and Linda grew unhappy with what they described as "the wishy-washy, no-clear-rights-and-wrongs" perspective on Christianity they found in their parish.

When Charles's company transferred him to a city 250 miles away, Charles and Linda agreed to look for another church. In the new city the couple attended several different churches and finally settled on a Nazarene church, to which they have belonged ever since. Charles explains that they like the "discipline" of this church. "There is none of this 'maybe it's right, and maybe it's wrong' stuff." He appreciates the Nazarene opposition to "the sin of homosexuality," for example, and he likes the heavy emphasis on reading the Bible and "following exactly what it says without getting all tied up in guessing games about how this or that passage should be interpreted."

Charles and Linda also like the Nazarene requirement that members tithe—that is, give a full 10 percent of their income to the church. They appreciate that if you don't tithe you can't continue to belong to the church. "This means that everyone who's there really wants to be there. You don't have to put up with a bunch of people of weak faith who won't support the church."

Each decision to leave the Catholic Church is inseparably related to the unique experiences of particular individuals. Some leave out of anger and disappointment. Others leave out of boredom or because they have intellectual conflicts with the church. Still others leave because they are hurt or disillusioned. As the following chapter illustrates, however, countless alienated Catholics every year find themselves reconsidering, and for most it's primarily an affair of the heart. For equally unique reasons they decide to return to the church and find the experience to be one that brings joy and peace. It is to their stories that we now turn.

CHAPTER TWO

Returning to the Church for

Many Reasons

Just as people leave the Catholic Church for many reasons, so people return for a wonderfully wide variety of reasons, too. These include coming back to the church following a life crisis; upon learning that one's marital status is no cause for alienation from the church; as the result of an invitation from a friend or relative; following marriage and the birth of a child; or simply because, in maturity, a person reconsiders a choice to leave made in adolescence or young adulthood. Sometimes people return when they learn that disagreement with a particular official church teaching is no reason for complete alienation from the community of believers.

Sometimes lapsed Catholics come home when they realize that you don't have to be a perfect Catholic to be a Catholic.[1] Indeed, the church's official Code of Canon Law declares that once a person is baptized, he or she remains a Catholic until he or she formally declares otherwise. Sometimes a return to the church happens when an alienated Catholic decides to take the first step by forgiving the church for hurts suffered, whatever the specific cause. Occasionally reconciliation with the church happens when an ex-Catholic reads a book that addresses his or her situation, or when he or she is touched by witnessing a personal appearance by the pope or another prominent Catholic leader.

Paths back to the church are inseparable from each person's unique self and personal history. For some the return journey takes years; for others it can happen almost overnight. It's appropriate, therefore, that we begin this chapter with the story of a woman who, at the time of this writing, was "on the way" and still uncertain about the ultimate outcome of her seeking.

For some people there is a strong and important intellectual component to their search, and often they are pleased to discover that Catholicism has an intellectual tradition that is many centuries old, with many paths to explore. Sometimes today, too, personal contacts made through the Internet are instrumental in helping people reconnect with the church. Such was the case for Diane.

Diane

At age forty-one Diane is married and a university teacher and researcher in a mathematical/statistical field. She grew up in a

Catholic family, attended Catholic schools and Mass every Sunday. Looking back, however, she does not remember actually believing in God, even as a child. "God" just wasn't a concept she could relate to. Diane never said anything to anyone about her disbelief, however. She says that she went through the motions of being Catholic, but she resented the perception that she was being told what to think. She also resented having to listen to homilies in church that addressed in a negative way "secular humanism."

Growing up in an environment where everyone else "believed," and being "the shy, smart kid," she kept her disbelief and resentments to herself. She continued to "go through the motions" and even received the Sacrament of Confirmation. Feeling that she had to do all this fueled her resentment, however. She felt that the Catholic Church was trying to force her to accept a world view that she just did not accept.

As soon as Diane was away from home, at age eighteen, she stopped attending Mass. Even before that, however, she went to Mass but refused to participate verbally in the prayers of the liturgy because she would not give verbal assent to what she did not believe in. For over thirty years Diane wanted nothing to do with the church.

Diane has always been an avid reader, and two years prior to this interview, after reading almost nothing but science for a couple of years, she began reading widely in philosophy, mostly about the work of eighteenth-century philosophers and earlier. She discovered that much of philosophy written back then addressed the existence or nonexistence of God and the characteristics of God. At the time Diane found it amusing that philosophers would go to such lengths to discuss "nonexistent entities" and developing "wild theories."

Still, Diane's reading started her thinking about the many people she knows who are practicing Catholics, including her family, a priest, numerous people she works with, and several of her friends. Why, she wondered, could all these people "see God" when all she could see was nothing but "a material universe that for some reasons existed"? Then one day Diane decided to "surf the web and look up things about Catholicism . . . the religion that I grew up with." She decided to try to discover what it was that all these people believed, and why. Diane found it intriguing that so many people believed in something so "weird."

Eventually Diane ended up on a website with an active discussion forum. She began posting her own questions and messages, making it a point to be open about the fact that she did not even believe in God. To her quiet astonishment, the other people participating in the forum didn't seem to have much of a problem with her disbelief. She got into some long and involved discussions, one a six-week conversation about whether "immaterial" things exist. Diane's forum correspondent kept gently challenging her positions. After several weeks Diane accepted the possibility that "maybe it wasn't just matter and energy."

Diane also had long discussions with other people on the forum about topics related to morality with and without belief in God, about whether prayer makes any sense if you're not sure there is a God, and so forth. Most of these discussions took place by e-mail. Once Diane's e-mail communications went on at some length, and she was able to pour her heart out about some "very personal issues." Eventually her e-mail companions-on-the-way helped her to conclude that it was okay to "read a bit from Scripture." Then she decided that it would be okay to step inside a church and try to pray, even if she was unsure that there was "anybody" there.

Eventually Diane began to have moments when she thought that God was more than a "maybe." One thing led to another, and as of the time of this interview, she was having conversations with a priest knowledgeable about metaphysics and participating in a parish Rite of Christian Initiation of Adults (RCIA) group. Diane still doesn't know if she will return to the Catholic Church, but she is in the process of trying to figure it all out.

Beth

Sometimes it takes many years for a person to find his or her way back to the Catholic Church. For some people this journey is intimately related to family issues they grew up with, and sometimes the journey also includes experimentation with other religions and philosophies. Such was the case with Beth, who found her way back to the church only after many years of searching.

Widowed for five years, Beth, sixty, is a retired medical worker who grew up as the oldest of seven children. With a hearing handicap and extreme nearsightedness, as a child Beth was very shy. She attended both Catholic elementary and high schools. Because of her hearing difficulty, Beth attended college only years later, at age thirty-seven, after several surgeries improved her hearing.

When she was younger, Beth was sexually abused by "a strange uncle," and she feels that this added to her to low self-esteem and even to guilty feelings that contributed to her movement away from the church. In the early 1960s, at age eighteen, Beth left home and "just sort of drifted." She did not feel close to her parents, and she began searching—for what she wasn't sure. During these years, Beth says, her faith in God remained, but she had no connection to the church of her youth. Beth tried Protestant churches, but she didn't feel right there. She gave some thought to Jewish beliefs. Eventually Beth embraced theosophy, a movement that began in the late nineteenth century and in many ways foreshadowed the contemporary New Age movement, including its incorporation of elements from various Eastern religions.

Interestingly, her involvement with theosophy led Beth to reconsider Catholicism. She missed the Catholic "liturgies and rituals, they were so rich for me." By this time Beth was married to a man who had been married before and had adult children from his previous marriage. She had not been inside a Catholic church for many years, but one Lent she mentioned to a Catholic coworker that she would like to attend the Good Friday liturgy. Unfortunately, the coworker dismissed Beth's comment with the remark that the church had changed considerably since Beth left, and she wouldn't appreciate the liturgy the way it is now. Beth's coworker did not invite her to go with her to the Good Friday liturgy, and Beth felt sad about that. Not feeling like she really belonged there, she did not want to go by herself.

Later, Beth's mother died after a long illness, and Beth attended the Catholic funeral Mass. "I was appalled . . . almost outraged," she recalls. "The priest wore white vestments with butterfly patterns all over. The Communion rail was gone, and ditto for the confessionals. Things in the church had definitely changed since 1960!"

About a month later Beth attended a wedding in yet another Catholic parish, and for some reason she was deeply touched by being in a Catholic church again. By the time the wedding liturgy was over, she knew that she wanted to return to the church. The next day was Sunday, so Beth attended Mass, where she sat near the back. Unfamiliar with the "new" Mass, she didn't know what to do. After a month had gone by, however, Beth was certain that she wanted to come home. For some reason she made an appointment to see one of the priests who, at a distance, didn't seem especially approachable. But later, when she entered his office, "he welcomed me with open arms."

The priest invited Beth to "make an act of contrition," a simple expression of sorrow for past sins and failings. Beth told the priest about an irregularity in her marriage that she was concerned about, but it turned out to not be a big deal at all, and "he took care of it then and there." Beth's summary of this meeting: "He was truly the Good Shepherd to me."

A few months later Beth spoke with the priest again, telling him that she would like to do something to help out in the parish, perhaps do some office work. The priest sent Beth to see a nun who was on the parish staff, and she invited Beth to be both a lay Eucharistic minister (one who helps to distribute Communion during Mass) and one of the lectors (those who read aloud the scriptural readings during Mass). Beth was astonished that she would be asked to take on such special roles, but she was happy to do so.

Thirteen years later, Beth joined the Third Order of Franciscans, a Franciscan community for laypeople. She has been active in the Third Order for eleven years now, helping out both locally and, on occasion, on the national level. "I am very happy since I have returned to the church; my faith keeps me going. Now I make a good effort to educate myself about my faith, to understand and appreciate it, warts and all."

At the same time, Beth believes that her time away from the church was not entirely a negative experience. "I grew in the time I was away from the church," she says. "When I returned to the church it was because I wanted to be there, out of love for God, not a fear of hell. Sunday Mass, and daily when possible, is a joy for me, not an obligation, not a simple routine, not just by rote because my parents did this, and I have done it for years. I made a conscious decision to return to the arms of Mother Church, and it has brought me joy."

Bob

It is not unusual for a husband or wife to be instrumental in bringing someone back to the church. Most often, however, it is an active Catholic spouse who brings the other spouse back to the church, not by pressuring him or her to return but through the simple example of living a Catholic life. Far more unusual is the story of Bob, whose non-Catholic wife was the one who led him back to the church.

Growing up in the pre–World War II years in Nebraska, Bob was a "cradle Catholic." Between the ages of eighteen and forty-six, however, he had nothing to do with the church. Bob was in the U.S. Army during the war and served in Europe, where he recalls seeing many Catholic shrines and grottoes in the countryside. He didn't feel like he was living a particularly good life, however, and he didn't want to be a hypocrite, so he stayed away from the church.

After he left the Army in 1950, Bob concluded that he had "a hell of a drinking problem." Living in Idaho at the time, he became a member of Alcoholics Anonymous. Later he moved to Utah, and in 1966, at the age of forty-three, he was a volunteer sponsor for the AA group at the state penitentiary. Through his volunteer work he met a Catholic priest who became a friend. Bob never told the priest that he was a fallen-away Catholic, however. About the same time, Bob's wife said that she wanted to send their two children to the primary school run by the Mormons. "I told her I didn't want them to be taught a lot of fairy tales," Bob recalls. Bob's wife replied that she had always admired the kind of man he was, and she believed that the way he was brought up must have had something to do with that. She knew that Bob never went to church, but she felt that growing up Catholic must have been a good thing.

Bob explains that it was this was the beginning of his return to the Catholic Church. "My wife said that she would like to be a part of the Catholic Church, and I believe this was God working in my life to bring me back to the church." So Bob contacted his priest friend and told him about being a fallen-away Catholic. The priest was completely surprised, but he was happy to help Bob and his wife reconnect with the church. "I've been back now for thirty-three years," Bob says, "and I have thoroughly enjoyed it. Among other things, it gives me a feeling of continuity."

Margaret

It's not unusual for people to leave the church for easily understandable reasons, and sometimes they show the most inspiring courage when they return. In such cases, it's typical for the return to be not on the church's official terms but on the returnee's terms. Margaret is one example of this kind of coming home to the church.

At fifty-two Margaret is married and the mother of a six-year-old son, and she works as a bookkeeper. The youngest of five children, Margaret grew up Catholic while attending public schools. Her father rarely attended Mass with the family because of something that happened years earlier between him and a priest. Margaret never learned what exactly happened.

Margaret calls her family of origin "very dysfunctional." Because her mother abused her and her siblings, as a girl Margaret often prayed that her mother would die. In the parish religious education classes Margaret attended, the nuns taught that to think about doing something sinful was just as bad as actually doing it. "So," Margaret recalls, "I found out in first grade that I was going to hell." All the same, Margaret continued to attend Mass, and later she even taught religious education classes for mentally handicapped children.

Margaret's first marriage was abusive. Her husband beat her, and following a beating one day Margaret went to her parish church where she was kneeling in prayer before a statue of the Blessed Virgin. A nun who happened to be there noticed Margaret's condition and called a young priest with whom Margaret had worked while teaching religious education classes. Sitting in his office, Margaret listened in disbelief as the priest told her that the beatings from her husband were God's punishment for marrying a divorced Catholic. Margaret responded by telling the priest that she wanted both him and God to leave her alone.

All this happened about 1972, and at this point Margaret began to drink heavily and abuse drugs. "My life was insane. The only thing I did was make a good living. The rest was a shambles." Since 1984, however, Margaret has been a member of Alcoholics Anonymous. "I have found God again, but it was a real struggle."

Margaret's second marriage is a healthy one, and her husband is a devout Catholic, which helped her to return to the practice of her faith. Like many—in fact, most—Catholics, there are certain secondary church teachings that she does not agree with, including the prohibition against artificial forms of birth control and the tradition of a celibate priesthood. But she says with a wry smile that she is a case of "once a Catholic, always a Catholic."

Robert

Part of some people's journey away from and back to the church is a struggle with specific doctrines and beliefs. Sometimes it is important for these people to confront, for example, specific disagreements between Catholic and Protestant churches, some of which go back to the Protestant Reformation, more than five hundred years ago. It's as if they need to wrestle with history themselves and decide which side they believe is closer to the truth, before they can decide whether to return to the Catholic Church. Not infrequently, these people must struggle not just with doctrinal differences but with misunderstandings regarding the doctrines themselves.

Although his mother was a devout Catholic, Robert's father was not so devoted to his religion. It was a struggle for his mother to get everyone to Mass on Sunday. Robert never attended Catholic schools or any form of religious education, and he guesses this was because his mother didn't want to fight yet another battle with his father. Robert received his First Communion somewhat later than was typical at the time, but only because he began to ask why children younger than he were receiving Communion.

As a twelve-year-old, Robert decided that he wanted nothing to do with the Sacrament of Confirmation because he interpreted it to be a permanent promise to "serve God and the church he supposedly established." As a teenager, he believed that the church was nothing but "a device used by corrupt men to acquire money from stupid and gullible people." At the age of nineteen, however, Robert experienced a change of heart. Between the ages of nineteen and twenty-two, while a university student, he became involved with Protestant friends and organizations, and his doubts about Roman Catholicism, particularly certain doctrinal beliefs, kept him away from the church.

These doubts included the Catholic understanding of the authority of Sacred Tradition, the doctrines of the Immaculate Conception—that is, that Mary herself was conceived without being affected by Original Sin—and the Assumption of Mary directly into heaven at the end of her life on Earth. Robert also disagreed with the Catholic teaching on the unacceptability of artificial methods of birth control and the existence of Purgatory.

At the time, Robert also seems to have had problems with Catholicism because he thought that Catholics were required to pray to the saints, which is not true. Catholics are not required to pray to saints, although there is an ancient custom of asking the saints for their prayers on people's behalf. Robert also disagreed with the Catholic teaching that the fullness of Christ's church may be found in the Catholic Church while Protestant churches are deficient in this regard.

He found especially distasteful the sixteenth-century, post–Protestant Reformation Council of Trent's pronouncements that various Protestant beliefs were false and that anyone who accepted these beliefs was solemnly excommunicated from the community of faith, or "anathema"—a term meaning "accursed" that is used by Saint Paul against anyone who preaches a false gospel (Galatians 1:9, 1 Corinthians 16:22).[2]

Robert believed in the doctrine of transubstantiation—that the bread and wine of the Eucharist become, in substance, the actual body and blood of the risen Christ. But he believed that this was not just true in the Catholic Church but wherever Christians celebrated the Lord's Supper. "Strangely enough," he says, "none of these difficulties prompted me to leave the Roman Catholic Church." At this point, he felt that any church would present problems, and it was God's will for people to serve in whatever church they found themselves and not "shop around" for whatever suited their whims. Robert was also active in his parish community and did not wish to leave that behind.

Two reasons ultimately led to Robert leaving the Catholic Church at age twenty-two. First, he wanted to "be baptized as a believer." While he did not disagree with infant Baptism, he did not feel that he had been a real believer prior to his conversion at age nineteen. Catholicism does not practice rebaptism, however, so it was not possible for Robert to be baptized again as a Catholic.

Second, Robert found it objectionable that Catholic communities exclude Protestants from receiving Communion in Catholic churches. "I believed quite strongly that believers were obligated to make available the Lord's Supper to all believers who wished to participate. The prohibition against sharing the Lord's Supper with other Christians I found impossible to obey in good conscience." The primary reasons Robert joined a Baptist church was because the Baptists agreed to baptize him again, and they allowed anyone to receive Communion whether agreeing with their doctrines or not.

More than a few Protestants had been a positive influence on Robert, encouraging him to pray and to read the Bible. They also helped him to feel comfortable about discussing the Christian faith in social contexts. At this time, Robert found it "offensive" that such obviously good people and positive role models were excluded from receiving Communion in Catholic churches while, at the same time, "Catholics who engaged in premarital sex, publicly supported abortion, led openly homosexual lifestyles, regularly missed Mass, talked openly of repeatedly getting drunk for fun, taught that the miracles in the Bible were enthusiastic embellishments rather than actual events, declared themselves not to believe in God, Jesus, the Resurrection, or transubstantiation, and said they felt no remorse over any or all of these actions were admitted to Communion without trouble."

At this time Robert firmly believed that Jesus' teaching on not judging others and showing mercy to all was incompatible with refusing to allow Protestants to receive Communion in Catholic churches. In his heart, Robert thought of himself as a Protestant, yet he continued to attend Mass as if he were a Catholic, but without receiving Communion because he could not honestly say that he believed all that the church taught as being revealed by God. Sometimes he felt dishonest since he knew that others considered him to be a Catholic.

For years Robert criticized the Catholic Church for its negative perspective on non-Catholic Christians, but he felt that if he actually left the church, he would be guilty of the same fault. Between the ages of twenty-six and twenty-eight Robert considered himself to be a Protestant but he continued to attend Mass in a Catholic parish. In spite of his disagreements, however, he gradually found himself in agreement with Catholic positions on issues such as artificial contraception, abortion, capital punishment, the Sacrament of Reconciliation (Confession), the existence of Purgatory, and the practice of infant Baptism.

Simultaneously, Robert began to have doubts about the Protestant teaching that Scripture is the only source of revelation. Eventually he rejected this classic Protestant teaching. Not incidentally, along the way he also met a woman who is a devout Catholic, and they fell in love and married. After a year of marriage and many discussions, and observing a shift in Robert's beliefs, his wife pointed out that he had changed and should look at returning to the Catholic Church wholeheartedly. After discussion with a priest, Robert agreed.

At the same time, Robert continued to struggle with the Catholic dogmas on Mary being conceived in her mother's womb without being affected by Original Sin and the belief that at the end of her life Mary was "assumed" into heaven body and soul. Recently, however, he has come to trust the church's judgment on these teachings because, given the church's stand on various life issues, it seems to make sense to trust its teachings about Mary, as well.

Robert believes that his full return to the church can be attributed to the prayers of his mother and grandmother. But he also recognizes the important part played by other people. His youthful conversion from atheism to Christianity happened after he met a believing Christian of his own age group. His return to the Catholic Church came after his devoutly Catholic wife "took the time to listen to everything I had to say instead of trying to convert me and correct my errors."

Robert's story is a valuable one to learn from for anyone who wants to help those who are searching. At the same time, people return to the church in so many ways. Sometimes a return can only be attributed to the movements of grace. The next true story is a good example.

Thomas

Growing up Catholic, Thomas recalls fondly that he was an altar server for about eight years, from 1945 to 1953. Married in 1966, "things started going wrong," he says, "so I blamed religion and therefore stopped going to church and abandoned religion altogether."

After fourteen years of marriage, Thomas and his wife divorced. He felt lost and began wandering from one religious group to another, including the Jehovah's Witnesses and various other sectarian churches. Then: "All of a sudden, for no apparent reason, one Ash Wednesday in about 1990 I just went to Mass and have been going almost every day since."

Thomas has no explanation for this. "It just happened, and I find things are much better, and I have more blessings. I look forward to Mass and find I can be sure of God's continual assistance. I read the Bible and almost any religious literature I can get."

Prayer is now a big part of Thomas's life. "I have no doubt that if I had not taken my own failings out on the church the whole thing would have come together, and I would be far ahead of the situation today. I wasted a whole lot of years, but now I feel that I am in the right pew, so to speak."

There is an old saying, "Once a Catholic always a Catholic," and in many cases this proves to be true. Often you can take the person out of the church but you can't take the church out of the person. This seems to be the experience of Jay.

Jay

Now forty-seven, Jay is happily married to a physician after two previous marriages. He is the father of two girls and the grandfather of three. Jay's parents were not active in the church although they sent Jay and his younger sister to Mass on Sundays and to religious education classes.

For some fourteen years, Jay and his present wife—who also grew up Catholic—were members of an evangelical Protestant church. Jay says that it is "hard to explain," but all along he still "felt Catholic." Then, in 1998, Jay and his wife "began feeling uncomfortable in the evangelical church, for a number of reasons." Unsure of what to do about this, they talked it over, and the more they talked about it, "the more we kept coming back to Catholicism." Jay had read a book by a man who had been raised in an evangelical church, then converted to Catholicism as an adult, and "it just struck me that I missed it."

Jay and his wife met with a priest. They "felt good about him and about the parish," and soon they "made the leap." The priest explained to the couple that Jay's first marriage would need to be annulled before they could receive the sacraments, and Jay agreed that this would be a good idea. "If we believe that a marriage is a sacrament from God, it should be very difficult to undo." At the same time, Jay was impatient with the length of the annulment process, something that can vary considerably from place to place, depending on the number of annulments local diocesan offices are trying to cope with at any given time.

Coming back to the church has definitely been a homecoming process for Jay and his wife. He says that he feels "comfortable knowing that I am around people [both at Mass and in the neighborhood] with whom I share common beliefs, even if many of us don't put them all into practice."

Lawrence

Growing up Catholic in the Midwest, Lawrence attended Catholic schools in the 1940s. When he was ten he learned that there was no Santa Claus, "and by the time I was thirteen I had also given up on the Easter Bunny and God." His main interests became sports and girls. After high school, Lawrence had such a good time in college that he flunked out in 1957. For forty years, Lawrence said, from about 1950 to 1990, his faith was "only dimly present, if at all."

Later, accepted by another university, he completed his studies, graduated, and became a teacher. In June of 1959, Lawrence had his first anxiety attack, and his mental health began to decline. Along the way, Lawrence spent time in various psychiatric hospitals, and he has suffered from manic depression ever since, although today it is kept "nicely under control" by medications.

In 1974, while teaching, Lawrence discovered that many of his Christian students were praying for him, and they invited him to accompany them to a nondenominational church, which he did for one year. Later he began attending an evangelical church, where he remained for eight years. Then, in 1999, Lawrence's mother passed away, and for no apparent reason he found himself receiving Communion at her funeral Mass. Lawrence's daughter had been encouraging him to return to the Catholic Church, and on his and his wife's thirty-ninth wedding anniversary he received the Sacrament of Reconciliation (Confession), then received Communion. His journey back to the church was complete.

As all of these true stories illustrate, the road back to the church is virtually always unique to the person involved. But quite often the choice to return is just the beginning, especially for Catholics who grew up in the pre–Vatican II church and left prior to or soon after the mid-1960s. The next chapter shows—again through true stories from real people—that returning to a church that has changed can be either a pleasant or an unpleasant experience, or a blend of the two.

CHAPTER THREE

Discovering That the Church Changed

While You Were Away

In the experience of more than a few Catholics, especially those who grew up in the church and left prior to the 1970s, returning to the church can be loaded with surprises. They have heard, of course, that the Catholic Church has changed, and the Mass is now in English. They may even have experienced the post–Vatican II reformed liturgy by attending the occasional wedding or funeral. But isolated events like this don't prepare a returning

Catholic for the experience of participating in regular Sunday Masses, week after week, and for the significant transformation in everyday Catholic life and thinking that has taken place since Vatican II. Not only the Mass itself has changed but Catholic attitudes toward the Mass and its meaning in the context of Catholic life and spirituality as a whole have shifted.

Prior to the Second Vatican Council, the Catholic Church looked different in several key ways from what it looks like today. The most evident way the church was different was that the language of the Eucharist, or Mass, was Latin. Today, of course, in the overwhelming majority of instances the language of the Mass is the language of the locale. In English-speaking countries, the Mass is in English. In Spanish-speaking countries—or Spanish-speaking parts of predominantly English-speaking countries such as the United States—the Mass is in Spanish. In France and French-speaking parts of Canada, the Mass is in French. In Germany, the Mass is in German; in Japan the Mass is in Japanese; and so forth. There is an exception to this rule, however.

In the early 1990s Pope John Paul II gave permission for local bishops to approve the use of the pre–Vatican II Latin Mass in specific parishes. Especially in larger population areas, it is often possible to find one or two parishes where the Latin Mass is available, usually no more than once each Sunday. Most parish Masses are in the language of the local area.

The Mass in the local language isn't the only difference between today's Catholic Church and the church prior to Vatican II, however. There are numerous incidental differences in Catholic life and practice. Prior to Vatican II, Catholic morality emphasized a sort of legalistic view of sin. The predominant idea was that to commit a sin was to break a law, either a law of God or a law of the church. Since Vatican II, a major shift has taken place in Catholic understanding. The *Catechism of the Catholic Church* explains that sin is "a failure in genuine love for God and neighbor" (1849).

In other words, today Catholics tend to view sin primarily in *relational* terms. To sin is to violate or damage one's relationships with God and neighbor. Sin is a social reality, not a merely private or individualistic one. Sin erodes the quality of life in human relationships from families to communities, from countries to the worldwide community of nations. Sin harms marriages, and sin has an ill effect on how nations relate to one another. All down the line, sin makes it more difficult for people to live together and get along with one another. Grace, on the other hand—a word that refers to God's living presence and his sharing of his very self with us—heals relationships and brings people together.

Stephen decided to "give the Catholic Church another chance" after being involved with a small evangelical church for more than twenty years. He saw an ad in his local newspaper inviting people estranged from the Catholic Church to think about "coming home." As the ad also suggested, Stephen called the Catholic parish closest to his home and spoke with the woman responsible for the parish Rite of Christian Initiation for Adults (RCIA) program. She told Stephen that the RCIA was for people who had not been Catholic before. However, the parish was about to begin a new program for returning Catholics. The program was called "Coming Home," and Stephen would be most welcome to attend the first get-together for that program in a couple of weeks.

Stephen agreed to think about it. When the evening arrived for that first meeting, he took a deep breath, got in his car, drove to the parish hall, and—not without some nervousness—entered the room where the get-together was being held. Some thirty

people were already there. The room was standard church hall issue, with a kitchen at one end, waxed tile floor, and fluorescent
light fixtures.

Some people were seated on folding chairs, others stood chat-
ting in small groups. A long table with a large coffeemaker and
disposable cups attracted most. Stephen helped himself to coffee
and a cookie, then took a seat in the next to last of the ten rows
of chairs. Soon a woman moved to the front of the room and
called for everyone to find a seat so they could get started.

The woman introduced herself as Mary Ann, explained that
she was director of the parish RCIA and Coming Home programs, and extended a warm welcome to everyone. She said that
the main goal of that evening's get-together was to give those
who would like to do so a chance to tell their story, however each
one chose to understand that idea. Mary Ann said that she would
begin, and to Stephen's surprise she proceeded to tell her own
story of being away from the church for fifteen years, then of her
own coming-home experience.

Mary Ann explained that she was ahead of her time. Years before it became a big issue among Catholic feminists, she left the
church because she became angry that women could not become
priests. She decided she could not belong as long as what struck
her as such a great injustice existed in the Catholic Church.
Stephen noticed that several of the women in the group nodded
in agreement as Mary Ann said this.

Continuing, Mary Ann explained that as the years went by,
she realized that she simply did not feel at home in other
churches. She missed what she called "the feel and substance of
the Catholic experience." Eventually Mary Ann met with a sympathetic priest who helped her to reconcile her convictions about
the ordination of women and continuing participation in the life
of the Catholic Church.

"I realized," Mary Ann said, "that I had to admit that even though I think women should be eligible to become priests if they want to, I could be wrong. The only alternative is for me to claim personal infallibility, and that's something I do not want to do. Also, by walking away from the church I was saying, in effect, that unless the church measures up to my personal standards of perfection, I will have nothing to do with it. I remembered something Father Andrew Greeley said years ago: 'If you can find a perfect church go ahead and join it, but as soon as you do it won't be perfect anymore.' "

Mary Ann's opinion that the church should be willing to ordain women to the priesthood hasn't changed, but she has. She went on to say that she now believes in a certain kind of humility in the face of twenty centuries of Catholic history and tradition. It would be arrogant of her, she says, to insist that after all those centuries the church suddenly change its way of doing things overnight. It would be egocentric of her, she adds, to require the church to ordain her to the priesthood as an absolute requirement for her to continue as an active member of the Catholic Church. "I'm now willing to leave this in God's hands," Mary Ann quips. "I'm sure that She will take care of it in Her own good time."

Members of the group smiled and chuckled appreciatively. A few expressed disagreement with Mary Ann's opinion that the church should ordain women who want to become priests. Others agreed with her. Mary Ann replied that this was a good illustration of how things are in the church today. "We can agree or disagree about this," she said, "but none of us needs to stomp out of the room; we can all remain together here and be on friendly terms even if we disagree about all kinds of issues that are, in the long run, going to change only in God's good time. And maybe they shouldn't change at all. Our perspectives can be very limited at any given historical moment. Only time will tell. The essentials of the faith, the heart of the matter, is what we share most deeply."

Stephen was impressed by Mary Ann's evident joy at having come home to the church and her relaxed, quiet willingness to accept the church where it is without demanding that it meet her expectations. Later that evening she compared being Catholic with being married. In a healthy marriage, she said, you need to learn to live with your spouse's quirks and imperfections, even his or her bad habits.

"Anyone who is married will tell you that his or her spouse does things that irritate you, but you don't give up on the marriage because of that. Sometimes the church is like that spouse who does things that irritate you. You tolerate things about the church that bother you because you love the church and you love the Catholic faith."

A man in the front row asked Mary Ann what she found most difficult about coming back to the church. She replied that although she left after the Second Vatican Council, in the late 1960s, many of the liturgical changes had not yet taken effect. When she returned in the mid-1980s it was almost like walking into a different church. "I was really mystified," she said. "Not only was the priest now facing the people, but laity were helping to distribute Communion, reading aloud the scriptural readings, and working in full-time parish ministries of various kinds." During Mass, she was surprised to see people standing to receive Communion rather than kneeling at a now nonexistent altar rail, receiving the consecrated bread in their hands instead of on extended tongue, and receiving the consecrated wine as well as the bread—something only the priest had done before!

Mary Ann was taken aback when priests readily admitted that they disagreed with official church teachings on a variety of issues, such as the prohibition of artificial contraceptives, and agreed that women should be eligible for ordination to the priesthood. "It took me a few months to get used to all this. I was also amazed when I heard homily after homily during Mass, and every one of them focused on the scriptural readings for the day."

Noticing that there were several mouths open in astonishment among the group, Mary Ann smiled and remarked that it looked like some of the things that surprised her were surprising others, as well. She then invited people to stand, move around a little, refresh their coffee cups, and regroup in ten minutes. Following the break, Mary Ann asked if anyone would like to share their story with the group. Several hands went up. She said that eventually everyone would get a chance, then she invited a woman toward the back to tell her story.

The woman appeared to be in her mid-forties. She introduced herself as Teresa, and she said that she had been away from the church ever since she was in high school. "I just stopped going to Mass and never even thought about coming back until recently."

Teresa explained that she and her husband, who was sitting next to her, had decided after much discussion that they needed to be involved in a church. Teresa grew up Catholic, but her husband came from a religiously indifferent family, and he was willing to look into the Catholic Church. "I knew that the church had changed, of course," Teresa said, "but I had no idea. Mary Ann, some of the things you've been saying are just amazing to me! I thought I knew what I'd be going back to, but I don't know. I liked the old Latin Mass, and I remember that it was kind of a special feeling to receive Communion kneeling down. It seems to me that shows more respect or something. . . ."

Mary Ann thanked Teresa for her comments and said that concerns like hers would be addressed in later sessions. "We can't do everything in one evening," she said, "but please know that your feelings and questions are important, and they will not be ignored. Also, I would be happy to meet with anyone during the week, prior to our next session, to discuss particular questions you may have."

Later that week Teresa called Mary Ann and asked if she could stop by, to which Mary Ann readily agreed. "How about if we get together for lunch?" she asked. The two women met at a nearby café, and over sandwiches they chatted briefly about mutual interests. Then Mary Ann asked, "So, did you have a question from the other night that you wanted to ask about?"

"Yes," Teresa said. "It's just that I have this feeling that if my husband and I return to the Catholic Church, we'll be returning to a church I'll have a hard time recognizing. I don't know if I want to do that. How can the church have changed so much from the way it was all those centuries?"

Mary Ann replied, "It may seem that the church has changed, I know, and in some ways it has. But the ways the church has changed are actually rather superficial. It's the incidentals that have changed, not the essence, and really, the church you remember had only been around for about five hundred years, since the Protestant Reformation in the mid-sixteenth century. The pre–Vatican II church was a Counter-Reformation church, a church on the defensive that placed a great deal of emphasis on structures, laws, and formal ways of doing things for the sake of holding the church together after the Protestant Reformation.

"Since Vatican II, we've tried to get back to our roots, back to the spirit of the ancient church insofar as we can. The Mass today seems very different from the pre–Vatican II Latin Mass, but it's much more like the Mass that the early Christians experienced. The fact is that the heart of the Mass hasn't changed. Instead, the 'new' Mass allows what the Mass is all about, and has always been all about, to come across better than it did before. I know it seems strange and different, almost like a different church, but with a little experience and a willingness to learn about the Mass you'll see that it all makes good sense."

Teresa thanked Mary Ann, and she agreed to give it a chance. She said that she and her husband would gladly return for the second session next week.

The changes in the church since the Second Vatican Council are many, but the word "changes" may be rather misleading—and too limited a notion—if we want to understand what has happened in the church since the mid-1960s. Pope John XXIII, the pope who called and convened the council, is famous for saying that he wanted the council to open the church's windows and let some fresh air come in. The Italian term he used was *aggiornamento,* or "renewal." The idea was for there to be a new springtime in the church, a rejuvenation and a getting back to basics, so the church could become once again what it was meant to be: a lively, living community of faith rather than a museum.

Even a cursory glance at the history of the church since Vatican II reveals, of course, that all has not been peace and concord. Inadequate as it certainly is to talk in such terms, because it tends to put things in overly simplistic terms, one of the main characteristics of the church today is a division between conservative/traditionalist and liberal/progressive Catholics. Most Catholics are more moderate than conservative or liberal, of course, but much of the *Sturm und Drang,* or turmoil, in the church today can be traced to disagreements between Catholics with basically conservative or liberal perspectives, and both groups sometimes can get quite emotional about their convictions.

There are conservative, moderate, and liberal positions on everything in the church from liturgical issues to the exercise of the teaching authority of the church; from how bishops should be chosen to whether women should be eligible for ordination to the priesthood. Someone returning to the church after as few as ten years away is likely to be startled by how widespread these disagreements are. From many local parishes to the offices of the Vatican, disagreements over such issues is a characteristic of Catholic life today. For someone who is "coming home" to the church, however, it is important not to misinterpret these signs of conflict.

Yes, there is widespread bickering in the church today over all kinds of issues. But most parishes get along pretty well. The truth is that turmoil in the church today is not a negative thing. Rather, it's a sign of life and a sign of hope. You have all these Catholics, these countless well-meaning souls, who care so much about the church that they are ready and willing to argue their point of view. It is perfectly legitimate to view the turmoil in the church today as being like labor pains. The church is being reborn, and a certain amount of struggle and effort is necessary for a reborn and renewed church to come into existence.

It may be helpful, however, to focus on certain aspects of church life that may come as a surprise to someone returning to the church after having been away since the early 1960s (or before) to the mid-1970s.

The differences in the church that will be most noticeable to a returning Catholic are the differences in the Mass, or Eucharist. This, after all, to use a traditional phrase, is "the summit and source" of the church's life. Weekly participation in the Mass is where most Catholics most frequently come into contact with their church—or, rather, to be more accurate, this is where most Catholics together most frequently *become the church* in an explicit manner. This, indeed, is the key to understanding how Catholics understand the Mass today.

We do not "attend Mass" like people "attend" a concert, dramatic performance, or dance production. The people in the pews at Mass are not merely pious spectators, there to watch what goes on in the sanctuary area. Prior to the Second Vatican Council, Catholics often spoke of the need to "assist at" Mass. The assumption was that the priest was the one celebrating, or "saying," Mass, while the congregation observed and followed along with the prayers—being prayed by the priest and the altar servers—in a missal, a small book with the prayers of the Mass in it in both Latin and English.

Of course, after the priest received Communion, the congregation could then come forward to receive Communion, too, but only the consecrated bread, never the consecrated wine, which was reserved for the priest. This was the only moment in the Mass when the congregation did anything more than watch what the priest and "altar boys"—and they were always boys, never girls—were doing and follow the prayers in their personal missals.

Today everyone takes for granted that the entire assembly participates actively in the celebration of the Mass. Priest and congregation together say or sing the prayers of the Mass. A kind of rhythmic liturgical dialogue takes place, back and forth between the priest and the congregation. Members of the congregation, men and women, serve as lectors, proclaiming the word of God in the first one or two readings from the lectionary and leading the responsorial psalm for the entire assembly.

A member of the congregation also leads the congregation in the Prayers of the Faithful, just before the focus of the Mass shifts from the lectern, or *ambo,* to the altar table. Likewise, women and men—called, technically, "extraordinary ministers of the Eucharist"—assist the priest with the distribution of Holy Communion, both the consecrated bread and the consecrated wine that have become the whole person of the risen Christ.

Returning Catholics do well to realize that the switch from Latin to English, while important to making the Mass more meaningful for everyone, was not a big deal. On a deeper level, the main difference today is that the Mass is a prayerful action that the entire assembly is expected to participate in. Here there are no mere spectators. That's the key to understanding why the Mass seems so different from what it was prior to the Second Vatican Council.

It's worth noting here, too, that many Catholics today are becoming more theologically sophisticated concerning their understanding of what it means when we say that the bread and wine become, in substance, the body and blood of Christ. The traditional phrase used to explain this mystery says that the bread and wine become "the Body and Blood, Soul and Divinity" of Christ. While this is not inaccurate, it doesn't do complete justice to the reality.

An explanation that is both theologically accurate, and that helps contemporary Catholics connect better with the tremendous mystery at the heart of the Mass, relates the transformed bread and wine of the Mass with the ultimate Christian mystery, namely, the Resurrection of Jesus. Thus: In the consecrated bread and wine of the eucharist we receive the body and blood of the *risen* Christ. We're not talking about "body and blood" as we experience them in ourselves and other people. Rather, we're talking about "body and blood" that have been transformed by Resurrection, an experience that boggles the human intellect. It is *this* "Body and Blood, Soul and Divinity" of Christ that we receive in Holy Communion.

It can be helpful to understand that "body and blood" as it is used in the Gospels is an ancient Semitic phrase meaning "the whole person." So when we say that we receive the "body and blood" of Christ in Communion, we're simply saying that we receive his *whole person*. This helps us to sidestep crude, gruesome notions of ritual cannibalism, too. So our summary phrase would be something like this: *In the Mass the bread and wine, while retaining the appearance of bread and wine, become in substance and in reality the whole person of the risen Christ, and this is the Lord Jesus we receive in Holy Communion.*

This understanding of the Eucharistic mystery is still in the process of being grasped and incorporated into Catholic spirituality, so returning Catholics need not feel like they are entirely playing catch-up on this subject. If anything, returning Catholics who grasp this renewed understanding of Holy Communion may find themselves one step ahead of many of their fellow Catholics.

Another aspect of Catholic life that may surprise returning Catholics is the post–Vatican II emphasis on the value and importance of the Scriptures in the life of the church. For many generations Catholics were not encouraged to read the Bible. Since the mid-sixteenth-century Protestant Reformation, emphasis on the Bible had become "a Protestant thing"—just as, for Protestants, liturgical forms of worship became "a Catholic thing." Most Catholics had little familiarity with the Scriptures, and even today this is generally true. This is unfortunate, but it need not be the case. Indeed, many official church documents—including the documents of Vatican II and the *Catechism of the Catholic Church,* not to mention many others of lesser authority—urge Catholics to become a people of the Scriptures, steeped in the word of God.

Returning Catholics may be struck by how the church's liturgical life is permeated by the Scriptures. This fact has not carried over into a big interest in the Scriptures in the average Catholic's everyday life, but returning Catholics should know that the Catholic Church firmly endorses the words of Saint Jerome (ca. 342–420), the most important Bible scholar from the church's early centuries: "To be ignorant of the Scriptures is not to know Christ."

Returning Catholics also will notice that some Catholic

terminology has changed. This is true, for example, for what used to be called "the Sacrament of Penance." While many Catholics still speak of "going to Confession," officially this sacrament is now called "Reconciliation." The switch from one term to the other reflects the post–Vatican II theological conviction that reconciliation between the person and God, and the person and the faith community, is what this sacrament is mainly about. Returning Catholics will notice that—in spite of Hollywood's continued fascination with the old darkened confessional "box"—in most parishes the setting for this sacrament is a small, informal "Reconciliation Room" where people may either kneel with a privacy screen between them and the priest or sit in a chair facing the priest.

In past decades there were rather strict requirements about "going to Confession" at certain set times, such as before receiving Communion if you were in "a state of mortal sin," and a great many Catholics "went to Confession" on a weekly basis, often on Saturday evening prior to attending Mass the next day. The long lines of people waiting in parish churches on Saturday evenings to "go to Confession" are a thing of the past because most Catholics don't receive the Sacrament of Reconciliation more than a few times each year—if that often.

The Sacrament of Reconciliation is in a kind of limbo for many Catholics today because they aren't sure what it is and how it fits into their faith and spirituality. It remains to be seen how Reconciliation will take shape as a part of Catholic life for future generations. Returning Catholics, however, should be aware that when it comes to "going to Confession," things are definitely different from what they had been.

If you are a returning Catholic and find yourself mystified or perplexed by ways that the church seems different, you might want to ask yourself: Why do I feel this way? That you don't know quite how to relate to the changes in the church since you last participated in the life of a parish may suggest that all along you have had an understanding of the church that precluded change. You may have been living with the presumption that the church was—and is supposed to be—virtually unchangeable, a static institution set up by God a certain way and meant to be that way permanently.

This is a good illustration of how we each have a kind of personal theology that we don't often think about. Just below the conscious level we each have a set of basic theological assumptions according to which we consciously gauge or evaluate anything having to do with faith, religion, or spirituality. Thus, these theological assumptions are the source of any surprise we may experience in the face of differences or changes we find in the church upon our return. The most obvious assumption behind our surprise may be the idea that the church is supposed to remain virtually unchanging. This is an assumption that no one can disprove; neither can anyone prove it. It's just there—an assumption.

We can ask ourselves, however, whether it is reasonable to continue making this assumption. If we look at the world around us, if we examine the historical record, if we consult our own personal experience, we discover that wherever we find life we find change. Anything that is alive is also changing. This is true in the natural world; in fact, it's true of the Earth as a whole. It's true of individual persons, and it's true of communities of all kinds. It's true of plants and animals. It's true of institutions, from governments to schools, and from charitable organizations to . . . churches. Nothing that is alive remains the same.

Even a cursory look at this history of the Catholic Church reveals that change has been a characteristic of the church's life since its beginnings, some two thousand years ago. The church that existed in the year 100 looks considerably different from the church that existed in the year 1000. The church that existed in the sixteenth century looks different from the church that existed in the nineteenth century. The assumption that the church should remain the same came, for the most part, from the fact that prior to the Second Vatican Council, for about five hundred years the church had not changed very much.

Since the Protestant Reformation and the Catholic Counter-Reformation that followed, the church had felt the need to raise the drawbridges and batten down the hatches, to mix a couple of metaphors. The church felt the need to protect and preserve itself as an institution, to get things under control precisely as a way to counteract and correct the corruption and abuses that sparked the Reformation. Five hundred years later, however, the Second Vatican Council was about opening some windows so a spirit of new life could fill the church from the inside out. In other words, most of the differences in today's Catholic Church are merely differences between the church of the last five hundred years and the church as it existed for some fifteen hundred years prior to that.

John Henry Cardinal Newman, the great nineteenth-century English convert and theologian, offered considerable wisdom in a book first published in 1878 titled *An Essay on the Development of Christian Doctrine*. "Nay," Newman wrote, "one cause of corruption in religion is the refusal to follow the course of doctrine as it moves on, and an obstinacy in the notions of the past."[1]

In the same book, Newman wrote words that are even more to the point: "In a higher world it is otherwise; but here below to live is to change, and to be perfect is to have changed often."[2]

In other words, because the church is very much alive, it has changed and will continue to change, because each new era needs to find new ways to express the same eternal truths. The heart of the matter remains the same, but the ways of giving expression to it can, do, and should change.

Feelings can be mixed, however, upon discovering that the church of one's past is gone, and it's important to admit those feelings and deal with them honestly and openly. The mix of feelings can be even more difficult to cope with if the returning Catholic has some anger about past experiences with the church.

CHAPTER FOUR

Letting Go of Anger, Bitterness,

and Disappointment

It's not unusual for returning Catholics, no matter how strongly they feel about coming home to the church, to discover that they have residual feelings they need to deal with as a part of the process of reconciliation. People who came to a parting of the ways with the church over issues related to divorce and remarriage may find that they still resent church policies—former or current—on remarriage. Individuals who were victims of pedophilia may still be angry for various perfectly legitimate reasons. The same is true for those who left the church as a result of other unpleasant experiences in childhood—in a Catholic school, for example—or as adults. If the person is aware of these feelings, most of the time they can be dealt with in a positive, mature fashion. In some instances, however, feelings of anger, bitterness, or disappointment may not be entirely on a conscious level.

Reconciliation between the person and the church may require the alienated Catholic to face feelings of anger, bitterness, or disappointment that he or she is or is not fully aware of. Regardless of how justified these feelings may be, they can be self-defeating and get in the way of a wholehearted reunion between the returning Catholic and the church. The Gospel of Jesus invites everyone to act like grown-ups, and Catholicism is in the service of the Gospel. Therefore, a return to the church may include a need to come to a deeper understanding of what an adult faith looks like, for this is the kind of faith that all Catholics, including those "coming home," are called to cultivate.

After seventeen years of involvement with a Christian sect rooted in biblical fundamentalism, and after a long period of studying church history and reading Catholic books on the Bible, Bill decided to return to the Catholic Church in which he was raised and spent his young adulthood. Deeply grateful for the grace of returning, at the same time he realized that he still had some feelings of resentment and bitterness because his final choice to leave the church seventeen years ago was sparked by the insensitive reception he received when he tried to talk with a parish priest.

Bill approached the priest, an older man, with questions about apparent conflicts between Catholic doctrines and what he found in the New Testament. The priest refused to discuss Bill's questions, telling him his questions were "stupid" and that as a Catholic he had no business trying to interpret the Bible on his own, anyway. Insulted, soon thereafter Bill decided that he had no choice but to leave the church if he wanted to be a true Christian.

Years later Bill realized that the priest could not respond to his questions about the Bible because he was not qualified to do so. Bill had made the understandable mistake of assuming that any parish priest would be well educated and informed about the Bible. Now he realizes that—unfortunately—sometimes this is not so, particularly in the case of older priests whose seminary education included little if any Bible study.

Some returning Catholics who have residual anger to deal with often find it helpful to seek assistance from a professional counselor or spiritual guide. Marta, who earned a degree in spiritual direction, has helped numerous returning Catholics to understand and deal creatively with their feelings of anger and bitterness. She tells the story of a woman named Rose, who wanted to return to the church but was still very angry about a priest who years ago had told her she was a bad person for being divorced and for remarrying outside the church and not having her children baptized.

Marta asked the woman to write a letter to the priest telling him honestly about all her thoughts and feelings. The letter would never be mailed—indeed, the priest had died years ago— but it would give Rose a chance to express her feelings instead of keeping them bottled up inside where they had been for so many years. The letter turned out to be about ten pages long, and it helped Rose to release her anger. Later, after Rose explained how writing the letter had been therapeutic, Marta asked her to burn the letter as a way of ritualizing her desire to not live with her anger any longer. Rose and Marta went outside, and Rose put the letter in a small trash can. She then struck a match and touched the flame to the letter. As the pages burned, she and Marta together read a prayer asking for release from anger and for healing.

"You have to understand," Marta says, "that anger over past hurts related to the church can be particularly insidious. People who have such feelings and are alienated from the church tend to generalize from the one person who hurt them, or from the one area of church life—such as regulations concerning divorce and remarriage—to the church as a whole, every dimension of the church's life and doctrines.

"Sometimes it can be difficult to see that the church isn't perfect, just as you yourself are not perfect. Maybe in the past you have said or done stupid things, or you have been cruel to someone. This does not make you a totally bad person, through and through. In the same way, because one priest or nun was mean to you, or one area of the church's regulations failed to reflect the compassion of Christ, this does not make the whole church totally bad or cruel.

"Much of the work I do with people who are angry at the church involves helping them to grow up in terms of their relationship with the church. I try to help them let go of unrealistic expectations with regard to the church, and often that's all that it takes to make it possible for them to come home. It may sound simple, but sometimes it can be a very difficult and painful process before healing can begin."

Away from the church since the mid-1960s, Katherine returned in the early 1990s. One of the biggest hurdles she had to surmount was anger at the church that she had lived with for some thirty years. When Katherine and her husband married, doctors told her that she would be unable to have any children, but later she did become pregnant. After the birth of her child, Katherine's doctor told her that if she became pregnant again she could die. When Katherine discussed the situation with a priest, he told her that she could not take oral contraceptives, even if the primary purpose was to regulate her menstrual periods. He said that Katherine and her husband would have to abstain completely from sexual intercourse. At this time she severed all contact with the church. Katherine stayed away from the church even through a later battle with cancer.

Along the way, Katherine started attending services at the chapel of an evangelical Protestant sect, and she became comfortable with that experience. Years later, however, her husband, Bob, went to his hometown to attend the funeral of his mother, a lifelong practicing Catholic. When he returned, he told Katherine that he wanted to return to the church. Katherine decided that it would be "nice to share a religious experience with my husband."

Katherine phoned a local parish and made an appointment to talk with the priest. When the two met, Katherine explained that she was "involved with Calvary Chapel and what had happened with my husband." She also said that while she believed that Holy Communion was "very special," she did not believe that it was the "real body and blood" of Christ. The priest said that Katherine was welcome to come to Mass but she should not receive Communion. This angered her, and she declared that she would never enter a Catholic church again.

Some time later Bob's sister visited for Christmas, and she and Bob attended Mass while Katherine stayed home. They came back with a parish bulletin in which there was an announcement about a session to be held for returning Catholics. Bob asked Katherine to call and ask about this, which she did. She talked with Norma, the woman in charge of the session, who invited Katherine and her husband to attend.

Katherine and Bob did attend a few meetings, but she "was still too angry with the church." The woman in charge of the program asked to interview them before they left, and they agreed. During this meeting, Katherine and Norma connected when Norma mentioned that she had recently been diagnosed with cancer. Although Katherine and Bob stopped attending the returning Catholics sessions, the two women continued to meet now and then, but they discussed nothing having to do with the church.

Then in 1990 Katherine and Bob visited Ireland, and a relative invited the couple to their house for a party, a going-on-sabbatical get-together for a priest in the family, and some seventy cousins would gather for the occasion. "But there was a hitch," Katherine said. The priest was going to preside at a home Mass.

Katherine had no desire to attend a Mass, so she suggested to Bob that they arrive late and miss it. "The Irish aren't known for punctuality," Katherine said, "so even though Bob and I arrived late, we were right on time for Mass, and we were given seats right smack in front." The priest presided at Mass so as to make it a warm and personal experience for everyone, including the relatives from the United States. He commented that it was no accident that Katherine and Bob were there.

When it came time for Communion, Katherine didn't know what to do. This was the last situation she had wanted to find herself in. When the priest offered Katherine Communion, he addressed the ritual words to her personally: "The body of Christ, Katherine." The ritual response is supposed to be "Amen," but Katherine replied, "Thank you." "Something happened that day," she said. She became very emotional and even though she thinks of herself as a person who doesn't cry, she had to choke back the tears.

Upon her return to America, Katherine called Norma and explained that something "weird" had happened to her in Ireland. Beginning that September, Katherine again began attending the returning Catholics sessions. The week before the beginning of Advent—which is the beginning of a new liturgical year and the season leading up to Christmas—Katherine entered a Catholic church for the for the first time in twenty-five years. About this time she also decided that she should receive the Sacrament of Reconciliation (Confession). When she explained to the priest that she had been away from the church for twenty-five years, she said that he "blew me away" by extending a warm welcome back.

Still, Katherine's anger at the church had not gone away. A priest counselor suggested that she visualize putting her anger in a balloon and letting it go, up and away. "But I couldn't let go of it on my own." Finally she visualized Jesus putting his hand on her hand, and she was able to let go of the balloon.

That year Katherine sent a Christmas card to her relatives in Ireland and included a note explaining that the Mass she had attended there had helped her to return to the church. In a reply, Katherine received the address of the priest who had presided at that Mass. He was in Chicago now, on his sabbatical. Katherine wrote to him, and at Easter he visited Katherine and Bob at their home in California, where he again presided at a home Mass.

Since that time Katherine's spirituality has deepened steadily. She worked on the returning Catholics team for two years, then she served on the Rite of Christian Initiation for Adults team for eight years. Today she is both a lector, proclaiming the Scriptures at daily Mass, and a lay Eucharistic minister, assisting the priest in distributing Communion at Mass and taking Communion to people unable to attend Mass. She is now learning to be a spiritual mentor.

Katherine adds that the Catholic belief she had the most difficulty with was belief in the real presence, that is, that Christ is truly and fully present in the consecrated bread and wine at Mass, "Body and Blood, Soul and Divinity," to use the traditional phrase. Katherine's priest friend helped her by using the love for the Scriptures she got from her involvement with the sectarian Christian church. He asked her to read chapter 6 of the Gospel of John:

> Jesus said to them, "Amen, amen, I say to you, unless you eat the flesh of the Son of Man and drink his blood, you do not have life within you. Whoever eats my flesh and drinks my blood has eternal life, and I will raise him on the last day. For my flesh is true food, and my blood is true drink. Whoever eats my flesh and drinks my blood remains in me and I in him. Just as the living Father sent me and I have life because of the Father, so also the one who feeds on me will have life because of me." (6:53–57)

The priest also suggested that Katherine compare the Eucharist to loving sexual intercourse in marriage, "two becoming one," and this idea made sense to her. Then one day at Mass, Katherine said, after she received Communion, she "just knew it was real." This, she said, was the moment when she finally felt completely free of the anger at the church that she had carried for so many years.

Frequently, when anger and resentment at "the church" have been the bases of a person's estrangement from the Catholic community, the key to beginning reconciliation is for an official representative of the church to express regret and ask forgiveness. At the same time, often the returning Catholic eventually realizes that rarely can all the blame for an estrangement be placed on only one side. Sooner or later a mature adult with an adult faith begins to see that he or she was not without fault, that he or she contributed, too, to being alienated from the church.

As one returning Catholic said, "When I look back on my twelve years away from the church, I see that in some ways I was being childish, kind of throwing a temper tantrum. It's embarrassing to admit that, but I think it's true. Yes, I had to forgive the church for what a nun did to drive me away. But at the same time, I had to ask the church's forgiveness for reacting the way I did, especially for so many years."

Anger and resentment at the church is not an uncommon experience, especially among those who grew up Catholic in the 1950s and '60s. Being Catholic often includes anger, resentment, and disappointment with the church, some of its leaders, some of its teachings, and some aspects of its life on the local level. For such people being Catholic may well have included periods of time, sometimes years, away from the church, but ultimately it meant continuing to participate in the life of the church *in spite of* the negative aspects of their ongoing Catholic experience. In the long run, these are people who take seriously the insight that the church is both holy and sinful, and they have learned not to expect perfection from an imperfect church for they themselves are far from perfect.

Still, anger, resentment, and disappointment with the church are never easy to live with, regardless of their causes. Lyla is in her mid-forties, has been married for twenty years, and is the mother of two children, a boy age eighteen and a girl, fifteen. In addition to working part-time in a Catholic hospital, Lyla is exceptionally active in her parish, yet she has no difficulty recalling many reasons that she has felt anger and resentment at her church. She traces those feelings back to various experiences in her childhood.

Lyla's parents wanted her and her older brother to attend Catholic schools, but long waiting lists prevented either of them from doing so. They had to attend public schools, and at that time—in the early 1960s—children who attended parish religious education programs, rather than Catholic schools, were made to feel like "second-class citizens" in their parishes. Lyla's brother wanted to be an altar server, but because he did not attend the Catholic school he was not allowed to do so. Later, in spite of being an honor student, Lyla's brother was refused admittance to a Catholic high school, and the family suspected it was because he had not attended a Catholic elementary school.

Lyla recalls the social life of the parish she grew up in as being "very clannish and unfriendly." The priests were far from warm and outgoing, and at that time the option of simply shifting to another parish did not exist, as people were required to belong to the parish in which they lived geographically. Another parish would not accept you as a member if you did not live within its geographical boundaries.

Lyla recalls, too, that the nuns and priests tended to present "a very negative view of God." The God she heard about as a girl was a grim judge, and the priests and nuns "strongly emphasized our sinfulness." In spite of all the negativity, however, from growing up Catholic Lyla received "a deep love and reverence for the Eucharist." She always wanted to attend Mass in order to receive Communion. Still, all through her childhood, teenage, and young adult years she "felt like an outsider looking into the church."

Lyla attended a public high school, and she tried to be involved in her parish by participating in the activities of the parish youth group. Still, she felt uncomfortable around the church. In college, in the early 1970s, Lyla began to question the religious beliefs she had been taught, and adding to her discomfort was the "unfriendly and judging attitudes" she had experienced. She "became a nonpracticing Catholic." This was a time when, among Lyla's age group, it was almost fashionable to not attend Mass.

By the time the late 1970s came around, however, Lyla found herself wanting to return to the church, and it was the Mass and Holy Communion that drew her back. "I missed the Eucharist," she said. "Other Christian religions did not believe in the living presence of Christ in the Eucharist and did not celebrate the sacraments as Catholicism did." At the same time, however, Lyla developed a panic disorder that led to agoraphobia (an abnormal fear of open or public places).

Lyla received treatment for her disorder, and she and her husband, Victor, were married in a Catholic church in 1981. Subsequently she experienced many difficulties associated with trying to have children, including the death of a baby girl in the womb. Lyla and her husband spent years trying to arrange for a Christian burial for their unborn child but encountered resistance at every turn. "At the time, a stillborn child did not qualify for this honor!" As the years passed, every time July came around—the month in which Lyla's child died—she became depressed, feeling that something important had been left undone.

Only in 1998 was Lyla finally able to bring some closure to this situation. She wrote letters expressing her anger and hurt, which she mailed to the local Catholic Cemeteries office and to the bishop of her diocese. To her surprise, the bishop promptly wrote back apologizing for the way the burial of her baby had been handled. "He was extremely compassionate," Lyla recalled, "and gave me information about the Elizabeth Ministry [a ministry that supports women who have lost a child during pregnancy], and said that he would keep me and my family in his prayers."

The bishop's words touched Lyla deeply. Soon a representative of the Catholic Cemeteries office contacted her, offering to exhume her baby's remains and arrange for a "proper Catholic burial." Lyla thought about this for two years, and she consulted with a psychotherapist who supported her final decision to accept the offer.

The grave of Lyla's baby was opened, and she was allowed to be present when the remains were transferred from one casket to another, according to her wishes. She placed articles of clothing, a blanket, and several stuffed toy animals in the casket. "After eighteen years," she said, "I was finally able to have closure to this experience."

The following day a Mass was celebrated in the mausoleum of the cemetery with a priest from the Catholic Cemeteries office presiding and a priest from Lyla's parish concelebrating. Later Lyla shared her story with several nuns at the medical center where she works. In the obstetrics unit, a committee was formed that established an official procedure now being used when miscarriages and stillbirths occur.

Lyla experienced many complications during later pregnancies, and she always felt that the priests in her parish had little understanding and compassion for her and her family during these difficult and painful times. She was often unable to attend Mass, and instead of understanding she received lectures from the priests. She received virtually no support from her parish during these days. In the long run, however, instead of leaving the church, Lyla used her negative experiences with it to spark actions that would help women in situations similar to her own. Lyla became active, for example, in a ministry established to help and support women who were pregnant and abused.

One priest from whom Lyla did sense compassionate support was Father Smith, a man who had left the priesthood in the early 1970s to marry. Eleven years later his wife passed away, and he chose to return to the priesthood. Lyla said: "I believe that because he experienced much suffering in his life he is able to be compassionate and supportive to others, whereas many of the priests that I have encountered have led very sheltered lives, and because of their life experiences have not developed empathy and compassion to a higher degree."

Unlike other priests, who defended the actions of official representatives of the church, Father Smith accepted Lyla's anger at how she had been treated. As Father Smith counseled Lyla, he said something that struck her as most profound, an observation that has changed her thinking on the Catholic Church. He said that "the church is both very holy and very sinful." In other words, like many Catholics who have left and returned to the church, Lyla learned that it can be naive and unrealistic to expect the church's representatives to be anything more than imperfect human beings.

Today Lyla says that her parish is "extremely supportive. At times I have felt that the people have spun a cocoon of love around me and my family. At one time, the parish gave us money to pay for part of the medical bills my family incurred. Several time our family was brought food baskets from my women's guild during times when my son experienced medical problems and needed to be hospitalized. Our parish has been one of my main support systems during these past ten years. I have seen a more open, a friendlier and a more compassionate church develop during this time. I no longer feel like an outsider looking in but feel very much a part of the church."

Today Lyla's faith is that of an adult. She has seen both the dark side and the light side of her church. "I have watched the church grow up as I have grown from my experiences. I have learned that the church is a very nonperfect institution. It is holy and sinful!"

Sometimes the anger people feel is primarily an anger with God that results in a rejection of the church, as well. Today Sharon refers to herself as "a Catholic who was once estranged from the church and have returned. Today my faith is strong, and I am happy to be a part of the Catholic Church. I am involved in church ministry, and I am currently a student in a ministry formation program." Sharon has come a long way, however.

Sharon says that she "grew up with abuse, which includes sexual abuse." She was abused by her father, her older brother, and a parish priest. All along, Sharon felt a "special closeness with Jesus," but at the same time she "felt angry and bitter toward God the Father." In order to hang on to her faith, she "separated God." She loved and trusted Jesus, but she had such a dark, negative image of God the Father that she rejected that image. "I was terrified of Him and wanted nothing to do with Him."

While she still lived with her family, Sharon attended Mass on Sundays because she was given no choice. "I was there in body only; my spirit wasn't really connected." Later, after she moved out on her own, she decided to leave the church, and she gave up on faith. "I figured, 'Why go to church? What did faith do for me, anyway?' I still hurt. I couldn't worship and praise a God who I believed to be vengeful and indifferent to my pain and needs. I couldn't worship and praise a God I was afraid to love and trust."

Sharon cut off all contact with the church. "For me it wasn't so much an estrangement from the Catholic Church but an estrangement from God that led to my dropping out of the church." For about one year she stayed away from the church, and during that time her life became "really chaotic." She became severely depressed, and she was unable to function on a day-to-day basis. "I really didn't care if I lived or died." Then, in "total desperation," as "a last resort," she called on God for help.

Gradually Sharon found her way "back home to the church," where in 1991 she "experienced a joyous and blessed homecoming." In time she learned to open up to God and "accept and believe in Him as a loving and gentle Father. I welcomed Him as my Father. It has been ten years since I have returned home to my faith, to the church, to my God, and to myself. I am still learning to relate to the Father whom I don't know well. I come to know Him more each day. I may not fully know how to relate to Him, but I no longer doubt Him and His love. I grow more in love with Him all the time. I am glad to have God as my Father, and I am happy about my return to the church."

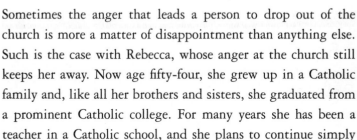

Sometimes the anger that leads a person to drop out of the church is more a matter of disappointment than anything else. Such is the case with Rebecca, whose anger at the church still keeps her away. Now age fifty-four, she grew up in a Catholic family and, like all her brothers and sisters, she graduated from a prominent Catholic college. For many years she has been a teacher in a Catholic school, and she plans to continue simply because she has been there for so long. Ten years ago, however, Rebecca severed her connections with the Catholic Church and joined a sectarian Christian church. She now believes that "God wants me to follow biblical principles and not traditions!!!!"

Rebecca says that she believes deeply in God, but she has a big problem with what she sees as the hypocrisy in the church. Some months prior to this interview, for example, Rebecca's son died from an asthma attack, and two weeks later she was diagnosed with breast cancer. Not one of the three priests in the parish where she teaches came to Rebecca to ask how she was doing after either of these difficult events. At the same time, Rebecca said, the pastors at the evangelical Protestant church she attends "have been in close contact with me and make sure I am surrounded by godly people and plenty of prayer coverage."

Along with the anger, bitterness, and disappointment returning Catholics may feel, for some their return to the church continues to be a source of conflict and stress because it means they must deal with a spouse's anger and resentment, as well. Dianne, for example, grew up Catholic and has "very positive" memories of those early years. She attended Catholic elementary and secondary schools and later graduated from a Catholic college with a degree in chemistry. She recalls that both she and her sister "wanted to be nuns." After high school Dianne's sister entered a religious order, and following college Dianne decided to join a contemplative religious order as well.

Dianne was happy in the monastery, but after six years she felt that God was calling her elsewhere. She left the monastery and went to work in the chemical industry. There she met and fell in love with "a wonderful physics graduate student" who was, and is, "a staunch Presbyterian." Six months after the two met they were married in an ecumenical wedding presided over by a Catholic priest and a Presbyterian minister. On Sundays the couple alternated between attending the Presbyterian worship service and the Catholic Mass.

Later Dianne returned to school to get a doctoral degree, and by the time she was working on her dissertation she was the mother of four-year-old and one-year-old children. She said: "Here I was trying to write a dissertation, with two small children in tow, going back and forth between two churches. I just needed to simplify my life. I was not angry at the pope or anything like that. I did not see anything very different about the Presbyterians, I was too busy with other things to really question it. I was never asked to take a course in Presbyterian theology. To be a Presbyterian it doesn't matter a whole lot what you believe, as long as you believe in Jesus Christ as your Lord and Savior."

Dianne's experience as a Presbyterian was, she says, "very positive." She grew in her knowledge of the Scriptures, and for twenty years she took an active part in the Christian education program and taught Sunday school for both youth and adult classes and filled leadership roles. She helped with the worship services and even gave the sermon when the pastor was absent. "These were the growing-up years for my three boys, as well as my maturing years as a spouse, parent, and professional. It was a very busy and energetic time."

Then one day, along with many fellow employees, Dianne lost her job due to a budget cut. Within a few months she found a new position as a university professor, but it required a ninety-mile commute from her home. Because this commute proved too demanding, she began to stay in an apartment near the university and returned home each weekend. Her church volunteer activities had to go, too. One thing this new arrangement left Dianne with during the week, however, was plenty of quiet and solitude. She recalled: "I began to pray. As my prayer life deepened, I experienced a strong desire for Holy Communion, something much stronger than I had ever experienced before. I asked my minister about this, and he was unable to help me. He suggested that if I wanted Communion I should present my case to the worship committee. I did so, explaining in the report why Communion should be part of every worship service. The worship committee evidently debated my request and wrote me a nice letter telling me that it wasn't the Presbyterian way. The minister was very kind, and he said that the committee members had no idea of where I was coming from. They simply didn't have the religious background for viewing Eucharist as such an integral part of church life and worship. That's when I realized that I was in the wrong place."

Dianne began her return to the Catholic Church by attending Mass on weekdays while she was away at her university teaching job. At the same time, she began to get spiritual direction from a community of nuns. Dianne's husband took her return to Catholicism "very hard," as he was firmly opposed to her return to the church. He accused her of betraying him and all of their Presbyterian friends. "His own Protestant upbringing and its attendant anti-Catholic bias all came to the fore with full force. He was antipope, antisacraments, anticlergy, etc." It was only after a Presbyterian minister told Dianne's husband that he had a crucifix in his study that he agreed to let Dianne place a crucifix in their home.

After about a year and a half of this ongoing struggle, a priest suggested to Dianne that should shouldn't continue to "straddle the line." She needed to make a decision to be Catholic or Presbyterian. Dianne already thought of herself as Catholic, but she decided to make it "official" by looking for a parish that would be pastorally sensitive to her Presbyterian husband. At each parish she considered, Dianne asked if her husband would be able to receive Communion with her. Catholic guidelines state that non-Catholics should not receive Communion because the Eucharist is a sign of unity, and as long as that unity does not exist it is inappropriate, at best, for Protestants to receive Communion in Catholic churches.

In one parish, however, perhaps because the priest was more able to understand the situation Dianne was trying to deal with, he told Dianne that it would be acceptable for her husband to receive Communion there. Dianne officially returned to the Catholic Church in this parish were the stress of her interfaith marriage would be lessened rather than increased.

Dianne explains why she was "very taken aback by the unhelpful attitude of most of the parish priests" she talked with about her "mixed" marriage: "The issue of mixed marriages was not addressed but quickly put aside as not important. For me personally and spiritually it is of the utmost importance. Four months ago, my husband and I participated in a Marriage Encounter weekend at a retreat house. It was a wonderful weekend, but the shadow of church separation cast its ugliness again. During that weekend the priest let us know that non-Catholics should not receive Communion. At the closing Mass, my husband was the only one who did not receive Communion. He has not been back to Mass with me since. How do you think that makes me feel? How do you think that makes him feel?"

For the sake of her marriage, today Dianne feels that she must lead a double life. She volunteers twice a month in the spiritual care department of a hospital, where she takes Holy Communion to the sick. She knows no one in her Catholic parish well enough to call by name or to call for help of any kind. All of her friends are Protestants, and most are Presbyterians. She attends Mass on Sundays, but she also goes with her husband to the Presbyterian worship service, and she is still counted as a member of the Presbyterian church. She considers herself to be a Catholic, "but I know that it is important to my husband, at this time, that I also be a Presbyterian with him."

Dianne does not like leading a double life. She finds it to be a great source of conflict and stress, but she can't see any resolution of her dilemma in the near future. She returned to the Catholic Church because she needs the sacramental life. "I need to live the mystery of Christ's death and resurrection on a number of different levels, and this is what the Catholic Church has to give. I need to experience reverence for the mystery of God and of my own creaturely self. The Catholic Church has a richness in its tradition that nurtures my soul. I long for something that the Catholic Church has the most promise of being able to help me find."

Dianne lives with the pain of being Catholic in a church that—at least on the local parish level—has little or no sympathy for the challenge of living in an interfaith marriage. "Someone looking at me from the outside would perhaps say that I am not a 'real Catholic' and not a 'real Protestant.'" Dianne describes her situation thus: "I'm doing my best in a difficult situation, and it's messy and fuzzy, and it hurts, yet it is my life the way it is. It is a life of faith and hope in God who I know loves me. My prayer is that all may be one. My prayer is that all may have peace."

One experience all returning Catholics share is that of reentry to a parish community after a typically long absence. Returning Catholics discover, to one degree or another and in various ways, that things have changed. In the next chapter we turn to what this reentry experience is like for returning Catholics.

CHAPTER FIVE

Becoming Active in the Life of

a Parish Again

Coming home to the Catholic Church is about reconnecting to a specific Catholic parish community. While the returning Catholic may have some issues that relate to the church as a whole, the most significant impact on his or her experience of coming home depends on the parish where the reconnection happens. A positive experience with a particular parish can make all the difference. Hence it's crucial for a returning Catholic to connect with a parish where he or she feels at home and welcome.

Catholic parish life today is characterized by considerable pluralism. There are urban, suburban, and rural parishes; poor parishes and affluent parishes; ethnic and ethnically mixed parishes; conservative, liberal, and middle-of-the-road parishes. There are big and small parishes, family-oriented parishes, and parishes made up of an aging population. There are parishes with no priest assigned full time, and there are parishes with high or low levels of lay involvement. Some parishes place an emphasis on "building community." Other parishes are less overt about this.

Perhaps the first thing returning Catholics need to keep in mind is that there is no "perfect" parish. I cannot repeat too often the words of Father Andrew Greeley: "If you can find a perfect church go ahead and join it, but as soon as you do it won't be perfect anymore." These words apply to parishes as well as to the church as a whole. You can look around for a parish where you feel "at home," but don't expect that parish to have perfect liturgies or be conflict free. All returning Catholics can do is find the parish that is the best fit for them and then make up their minds to live with the ways that parish falls short of their ideals.

At the same time, it's important for returning Catholics—as for those converting to Catholicism—to realize that the church they are reconnecting with is bigger than any particular parish community. Ultimately, one's membership is in the Catholic Church as a whole, not just with this or that parish. If a Catholic moves to a new city he or she remains a Catholic. This is one difference between a Catholic and a sectarian Protestant Christian or even a mainline Protestant Christian. Many Protestants think of the various Protestant denominations as more or less interchangeable. Not so for Catholics. The Catholic Church isn't interchangeable with any other church. The Catholic Church isn't merely one of the various Christian denominations. Catholic theologian George Weigle explains why the Catholic Church isn't just another denomination:

> A denomination is something we help create by joining it; according to Vatican II, however, the [Catholic] Church is a divinely instituted community into which we are incorporated by the sacraments of initiation (baptism, confirmation, the Eucharist). Denominations have members like voluntary associations or clubs; the Church has members as a human body has arms and legs, fingers and toes. A denomination has moving boundaries, doctrinally and morally; the Church, according to Vatican II, is nourished by creeds and moral convictions that clearly establish its boundaries. The structures of a denomination are something we can alter at will; the Church, according to Vatican II, has a form or structure, given to it by Christ. Catholicism has bishops and a ministerial priesthood, and Peter's successor, the Bishop of Rome, presides over the whole Church in charity, not because Catholics today think these are good ways to do things but because Christ wills these for his Church.[1]

Participation in the life of a parish community is not just participation in the life of that local Catholic community. It is also the way we participate in the life of the universal Catholic Church, so that no matter where the individual Catholic goes, he or she belongs to the church by belonging to a parish.

Prior to the Second Vatican Council, Catholic parishes were generally cut from the same cloth. Differences from one parish to the next were incidental. I recall one summer, when I was ten or eleven years old, visiting cousins who lived in a much larger city. While there, we attended Sunday Mass, and I was surprised to see the altar boys clad in bright red cassocks, whereas in our small-town parish, and every other parish I had ever visited before, ordinary black cassocks were the custom. Other than this, of course, the Mass in the big-city parish was identical to the Mass in every other parish.

In the decades following Vatican II, Catholic parish life became far more pluralistic. Most parishes can be characterized as middle of the road, but medium to large cities all seem to have their "liberal" and "conservative" parishes, too. In some parishes the liturgy on Sundays tends to be low key to dull. In other parishes Mass is more of a lively affair. In some parishes liturgy committees are heavily involved in planning Masses, and Masses on big feast days, such as Easter or Christmas, can take on the characteristics of a multimedia event that include slides or videos, liturgical dancers, and musical instruments you might not expect to hear in church. In other parishes the "liturgy committee" is the pastor, period. Conservative parishes stick rigidly to the official liturgical rules and regulations. Liberal parishes sometimes "push the envelope" as far as possible liturgically.

Some parishes have an active parish council that the pastor listens to and takes guidance from. Some parishes have a parish council, but it is primarily there to rubber-stamp decisions that the pastor makes. Some parishes have no parish council at all. Some parishes have many ministries and social and educational activities that involve people of all ages. Some have little going on beyond the regular Sunday Masses.

Given this situation in parishes today, it will come as no surprise that returning Catholics have a variety of experiences upon reentry to parish life. One thing that does seem to characterize the experience of returning Catholics in general is their high level of interest in being involved in their parish community. Similar to new converts, returning Catholics have a higher than average level of enthusiasm for getting involved in their parish.

Like many returning Catholics, Jim grew up Catholic and

attended Catholic elementary and secondary schools. His family was very observant, going to Mass every Sunday and all Holy Days. Jim's older brother entered the seminary but left after five years. His older sister became a nun but left after three years. Jim was never so inclined, but he nevertheless took his Catholic faith seriously. Then, in 1968 when Jim was almost twenty, his mother died of colon cancer.

Jim says that he "blamed God" for his mother's death, and that is why he "left the church." One month later Jim joined the Air Force. Three months after that he was married, and nine months later he became a father for the first time. During the six years Jim was in the Air Force he attended Mass only occasionally, though he and his wife did have their three children baptized, "although I'm not sure why," Jim says. Jim describes himself during these years as "a twice-a-year Catholic," attending Mass only on Christmas and Easter. Then he stopped going to Mass altogether.

After ten years, Jim's marriage ended in divorce. He met his present wife through his work, and he explains that he returned to the Catholic Church because of his wife's influence. She became a Catholic as a child and attended Catholic schools. Jim returned to the practice of the Catholic faith with their marriage. In the spring of 1993, Jim made a Cursillo Weekend (a faith renewal program for men and women) and has been active in his parish ever since. He explains: "After my return, it felt absolutely wonderful to become involved in my parish. I was working toward my MBA, so I didn't join the choir right away, but I was elected to the parish council (remember, this is a *small* parish, so any input is regarded as valuable input), and then, when I graduated, I joined the choir and have never looked back. . . .

"Surprises? Yes. Open-mindedness, acceptance, a welcoming and embracing environment in which to expand one's spiritual horizons, some really wonderful clergy and some terrible clergy (definitely a small minority amount, but still, one bad apple . . .) and, most important, an environment which nurtures a sense of humor and a sense of irony in one's faith journey."

Among the disappointments Jim says he has experienced since his return the main one has been in the church's hierarchy, "from the bishops on up." Among other things, he has a hard time with the hierarchy's "rants against the gay and lesbian lifestyles, their relegation of women to second-class citizenry, their arrogance to think of Catholicism as the *only* road to salvation, [and] their continued opposition to . . . birth control."

Jim has found that participation in the life of his parish requires a person to cultivate a genuinely adult faith, a faith that enjoys good times but is patient and puts down deeper roots during the not-so-good times. For example, Jim says, for several years his parish enjoyed the presence of a pastor everyone liked. Then, when he was transferred, the parish has had "a succession of mediocre priests." Jim learned that his faith could not depend on whether he likes a particular priest or not.

Jim believes that his experience of the ups and downs of parish life has helped his faith to grow. He now says that "God is present in each and every one of us and . . . we can choose to revel in that knowledge or to reject it; that's our call. If we choose to revel in it, we will simply be amazed at our capacity to help other people as well as ourselves."

Returning Catholics tend to be like the Catholic population at large in the sense that they may be progressive or conservative, happy with life in their parish or not so happy with it. The main characteristic returning Catholics seem to have in common is a desire to get back into parish life, deal with what they don't care for, and rejoice in what they find good and spiritually nourishing. If anything, returning Catholics may have a bit more capacity to be patient with a parish community.

Karla was away from the church for fifteen years, during which time she was involved with more than a few different Protestant churches. When she did return to the Catholic Church, she was surprised to find that many priests were "too liberal for my tastes." Some priests seemed to think that "we should all be on the bread line, giving everything away, some encouraging Eastern philosophy."

Karla was also uncomfortable with the degree of leadership many women exercise in their parishes and with their theological perspectives, "embracing New Age power to themselves, praying to goddesses." At the same time, she regretted seeing older priests who "faded into the background, giving women carte blanche."

It was disconcerting, Karla said, to watch as "decent people were driven from the church in disgust, defeat, and confusion, and as many were told to leave if they didn't like it—and so they did, an exodus into more conservative churches, and many never going to church again."

Feeling that it was worth being patient for, today Karla believes that there has been "an upheaval in many parishes." Today, however, she feels that "things have settled . . . the Power to Women idea having lost its steam . . . their goddesses could not help them. Finally the Pope's chosen men have surfaced from all over the world, placed in dioceses that were waning spiritually. Priests from all nations are pastoring churches in our state. A resurgence of spiritual renewal has sprung up in our parishes, pushing out the radical idealism of the New Age. Enter serenity, after these years of battle, taking back the church. Learning to walk in the ways of Christ, not on Sundays but every day, striving for His standard of excellence, while encouraging one another."

Experiences with parishes vary from one returning Catholic to another, yet one thing seems certain: The particular parish the returning Catholic associates with has a tremendous impact on the rebirth of his or her faith. While each one's story is unique, some stories seem to typify the most positive experiences shared by many returning Catholics. Marilyn, for example, is like many post–World War II baby boom Catholics. While the story of her growing-up years has its own unique aspects, the story of her actual return to parish life is far from atypical.

Marilyn was born in 1948 to a mother who was an inactive Catholic and a father who was an inactive Lutheran and "an alcoholic who could never keep a job." When he was drinking, he often beat Marilyn's mother and brother. "Early on, around the age of six, I began to pray to God that I wanted my father to die so that the abuse would stop. Prayers of this nature continued throughout my teens."

While her home life was turbulent, Marilyn found some stability and peace in the church. She attended catechism classes and received the Sacrament of Confirmation when she was in junior high school. She recalls many Easter Sundays as a girl when she would dress up with hat, gloves, and a corsage her mother always bought for Easter, and she and her brother would go to Mass by themselves. Marilyn's brother was an altar server, so she would sit by herself.

When she was in the fourth grade, Marilyn joined the parish choir, "and I enjoyed that immensely, singing 'Immaculate Mary' and other traditional songs." Today, many years later,

Marilyn is a song leader and a member of her parish's funeral choir, "and when I sing some of the old standbys I'm quickly transported back to those years!"

Later, in 1960, Marilyn's parents separated, and they lost their home to foreclosure. Marilyn's brother had married, so it was just she and her mother who moved in to live with Marilyn's maternal grandparents. "It was a most unsettling time, and I felt that God really didn't care about me or my family!"

Two years later Marilyn's parents reconciled, and her father joined his wife and daughter in the home of Marilyn's grandparents. It so happened that Marilyn's grandparents were longtime members of an ethnic Catholic parish, and Marilyn's grandmother had a strong effect on her. "She loved to go to 5:30 A.M. Mass. Because we lived in a rough neighborhood and I didn't want her walking alone, I accompanied her to Mass from the age of eighteen to the age of twenty-two. A lot more rubbed off on me during that time than I could ever imagine, but it took a lot of years for me to realize how important my faith and she were to me."

During this same time Marilyn's mother had begun to drink, too. Although her grandparents tried to keep life as normal as possible for her, Marilyn began to look for some way to escape. A few months after her eighteenth birthday, her father entered a hospital for some tests and died eleven days later, and Marilyn's mother's drinking increased. Marilyn couldn't understand why God would allow this situation to continue.

Marilyn graduated from high school and with veteran's benefits from her father she was able to attend college and, after much hard work, she completed her teaching degree. Then, in 1970, she married her high school sweetheart, who was also a marginal Catholic. They had a Catholic wedding, but the couple rarely attended Mass. "We struggled early on in our marriage with going to Mass and never got involved with any parish; we just sort of drifted. There were periods when we would make an attempt to attend, but more often we grew lazy and in growing lazy it became easier and easier not to make the effort."

After fifteen years, Marilyn's marriage "fell apart." The couple had a business, which Marilyn's ex-husband kept, though he soon went out of business. In 1986 the couple's divorce became final. At the same time Marilyn lost the house they had shared, and soon after that she lost her job. Marilyn recalled: "During that time I began to see that I couldn't do it alone. I felt lost and alone, without anything to anchor or guide me. Then, for some reason, I decided to go to daily Mass, sitting as close to the back [of the church] as I could. I sat in back for a couple of reasons. First, I was closer to the door and could make a fast exit if I needed to. I was experiencing panic attacks at that time. Second, by sitting in the back I could observe what others were doing and do likewise. I had missed the Vatican II changes so I wasn't too sure what I should do and when."

After attending daily Mass for about six months, a member of the parish who was the father of a friend of Marilyn's suggested that she talk to a priest. Like more than a few other divorced Catholics, she assumed that she could not longer receive Communion. The priest assured Marilyn that this was not the case, that she should continue to receive Communion. So Marilyn continued to attend daily Mass, though it was often a struggle for her. Eventually she celebrated the Sacrament of Reconciliation and began trying to catch up with the church, which seemed so different from the church of her youth.

In all of this, Marilyn found that it was the parish community she connected with that made all the difference. One morning at daily Mass, the priest asked her to be a Eucharistic minister (one of the laity who help the priest to distribute Communion). "How I struggled with feeling unworthy, thinking that if people knew what a sinner I was, they'd think the worst of me!"

This was the beginning, for Marilyn, of a real return to a parish community. Gradually she started attending Mass on Sundays, too, and she became "a regular." She still sat near the back of the church, "just not as far back!" Six months later Marilyn attended a special retreat for faith renewal. "I was so filled with the Spirit that I remember standing in front of the group saying 'I don't know what I'm called to do but I do know that this is not the end of it'—and it wasn't!"

Soon after this retreat, Marilyn began working for the foundation of a Catholic high school. At this time, she began reading and attending workshops to learn more about her Catholic faith. Following another faith renewal retreat, Marilyn applied to a parish for the position of religious education coordinator— and she was hired. "I became a sponge, just soaking up as much information as I could about my newly rediscovered religion. I often made a joke that after my name I should have, like the letters that members of religious communities have, 'J.C.L,' for Johnny-come-lately."

In 1991 Marilyn realized that she had inherited her parents' tendency to abuse alcohol, so she voluntarily entered a twenty-eight-day treatment program. She was honest with her extended family about where she was going. She also, for no apparent reason, informed the landlord of the apartment she had been renting that she would be moving. Yet she had no plans for another place to live. Once again she began to see how God can work through a network of parish relationships. The son of a fellow parishoner called to say that his mother would soon move into a nursing home. Would Marilyn be interested in buying her house?

Marilyn met with the man and told him about her earlier

bankruptcy. She had no idea how she could pay for a house. "He told me that he would work on some things to see if it was feasible. Would you believe that two days before I was released from treatment I received a large packet in the mail with the land contract paper to be signed. I didn't even have to come up with a down payment because he took my first three months' payments as the down payment. What a miracle! To this day when I see Ted I thank him for taking a chance on me. God is good!"

This was not the end of Marilyn's story of her return to the church, however. As it turned out, she became instrumental in her mother's return, as well. As Marilyn was herself coming home to the Catholic Church, she periodically traveled to the city where her mother lived to visit her. During each visit, Marilyn would make it a point to attend Mass. Before she became confined to a wheelchair, Marilyn's mother occasionally accompanied her daughter.

"I would sing and participate in the Mass," Marilyn recalled, "and I knew she was watching me. Finally one time she became interested in the missalette so I threw an extra buck in the collection basket and she took it home." About three months later, Marilyn's mother contacted the diocesan office and asked that a missalette be sent to her. She then began to use her missalette as she watched the Mass broadcast on television for shut-ins. One year for Christmas Marilyn gave her mother a prayer book, which she continues to use to this day.

"Talking about religion during our visits became a habit; she would often ask questions about the church, and since I was working for it she felt I was an expert. She now has rediscovered her roots in the Catholic Church and has felt a great sense of peace about it. . . . While it seems as if there'll always be a certain tension between us because of the many things left unsaid, there also seems to be a comfort level that both of us have found with each other. She now takes great pride in what I do."

Marilyn's return to the church and to a parish took on a relatively unusual dimension because of the extent to which she has become involved in church ministries, both personally and professionally. She now directs her parish's faith formation program and is a member of her diocese's team that offers introductory sessions on the Welcome Home program to parish teams. Recently she facilitated a Welcome Home session in a small rural parish. "What a touching afternoon that was. It renewed in me a sense of gratitude for all that I have and feel about being Catholic!"

The pastor of Marilyn's parish is an older man, so she tries to help out as much as she can. Some time ago he asked Marilyn to take responsibility for the parish's wake services for members of the parish who have passed away, and Marilyn did not hesitate to say yes. She also brought to her ministry a special sensitivity based on her own experience of being away from the church. In this sense, for Marilyn being away from the church turns out to have been a gift:

"Those experiences have allowed me to share with others in many ways but especially with those who are away from the church. I work hard at trying to put family and friends at ease; to explain our rituals and to give short introductions to the readings so that those listening may be more comfortable with what is going on. I remember many times feeling so out of place because I didn't have a clue what was going on."

For Marilyn especially, coming home to the church has meant identification with a parish that calls on her to be there for returning Catholics, to share with them her gift of being able to understand and sympathize because she herself has been where they are.

It's true that coming home to the Catholic Church is invariably linked to participation in the life of a parish community. But sometimes a returning Catholic makes this parish connection first through a particular individual, either a member of the parish or—as in Bob's case—through a priest. First, however, the story of how Bob happened to leave the church.

Bob grew up in a relatively poor Italian Catholic family and attended a public grade school. When it came time for high school, however, Bob won an athletic scholarship to a prestigious Catholic prep school for boys. "Was I intimidated!" Bob recalls. "You had to wear a suit and tie to school, so my older brother bought me a couple of outfits."

Unfortunately, this prep school was where Bob first experienced ethnic prejudice. Most of the other boys were from wealthy Irish Catholic families, and Bob was on the receiving end of ethnic slurs. "I wanted so much to fit in that I just took it with a smile."

After graduation, Bob attended a Catholic college for two months because the headmaster at the prep school had said that if the boys from his school didn't attend a Catholic college, the prep school had failed in its purpose. That college did not have the curriculum Bob wanted, however, so he dropped out and later enrolled at a secular university, where he earned degrees in health and physical education. Throughout his years in high school and college Bob continued to be a practicing Catholic.

Soon after he finished college, Bob decided to marry. His future wife was not Catholic, but she agreed to a Catholic wedding. When Bob went to the parish to get "the requisite papers to be married," the priest "blew his stack." Bob had just moved out of that parish so the priest told him to go to his new parish. When Bob did this, the new priest "was one step below nasty."

This priest didn't take care of the paperwork as he was supposed to, and Bob's wedding ended up being delayed as a result. "Thus began the seeds of my leaving the church."

After he was married, Bob continued to attend Mass, and when his two children were born he took them to Mass, as well. But: "I was starting to get disgusted with the priests ad-libbing the sermons." Bob's marriage was "unraveling," and he decided to "leave the church, as well."

For forty-one years, whenever anyone asked him about his religion, Bob called himself "a lapsed Catholic." During these many years, Bob attended Mass three times and "felt nothing." Occasionally he accompanied friends to Protestant services. "Terrific sermons, but meaningless liturgy," he recalls.

Eight years ago Bob moved to his present home to enjoy his retirement years. "I noticed that I always looked for Catholic articles in the religious section in Saturday's newspaper. I was afraid that if I went to Mass and heard the same old tired sermons I would never return." Catholic friends then told Bob about a priest who is pastor of the Catholic parish in the town where he now lives. "I went to five Masses in a row and loved it. I was afraid to go to Confession, but I wanted to receive Communion. So I went to Confession."

When Bob told the priest that he had not been to Mass in forty-one years, "he had a sort of astounded look on his face." This is what happened next: "About one fourth of the way through my litany of sins I had committed, he stopped me, came to me, and put his hands over my head and said, 'Christ has called you back.' Very emotional and cathartic moment for me."

The key for Bob's return to the church was a particular parish priest who does not give "the same old tired sermons" and who celebrated the Sacrament of Reconciliation in a sensitive, welcoming, pastoral manner. Today Bob's parish is basic to his life. "My life has really improved in the last few years. I no longer am tired of figuring out how I am going to amuse myself. I sing in the choir, am part of the prison ministry, volunteer in the soup kitchen, and am a mentor in the parish's ski program. I love going to Mass. When your spiritual life is in order I find wonderful things happening."

Recently Bob returned to the parish of his youth for the parish's 120th anniversary celebration. The priest who had blown his stack at Bob and his fiancée was there, and he and Bob enjoyed each other's company. "Still has all his marbles. We had a nice chat."

Sometimes the journey of a returning Catholic takes many twists and turns along the way. Almost inevitably, however, the final chapter in the story of his or her homecoming is about a coming to terms with an imperfect but graced parish community of one kind or another. Indeed, in retrospect the journey itself can be seen as an ongoing search for a parish community that the returning Catholic can call home.

Frances was "a cradle Catholic" who lost interest in the church during her teens and early twenties. During college Frances was sometimes approached by fellow students who tried to convert her to various forms of fundamentalist Christianity, but she wanted nothing to do with religion of any kind. "I regret that I avoided these people like the plague and in fact did not pursue any kind of religious life during my college years. I think I would have saved myself a lot of grief if I had, as I struggled with emotional problems and feelings of isolation from my classmates," she said.

Following graduation Frances went through a lengthy selection process for employment with the U.S. Department of State as a Foreign Service officer. Eventually, however, while stationed in foreign countries, she became chronically ill, both physically and mentally, which she attributes to a "dysfunctional" family background as well as biological and even spiritual causes. The State Department returned Frances to the United States, and during her final two years with the diplomatic corps she began to realize that "a relationship with God was the answer to many of my personal problems." She began to explore many different churches.

Frances participated in a lunch-hour Bible study group, and one day the text under consideration was Joshua 1:9, which reads: "I hereby command you: Be strong and courageous; do not be frightened or dismayed, for the LORD your God is with you wherever you go."

These words motivated Frances to begin taking prayer and a daily relationship with God more seriously. For a while she attended worship services at a Methodist church. Then one day she received a copy of "some kind of mailing" from a nearby Catholic parish, and she began going there. "They had two excellent priests there, and I felt like I had come home." Frances participated in the parish's program for returning Catholics and all seemed well.

The two priests that Frances liked were transferred to other parishes, however, and she didn't care for the priests who replaced them. About this time, she moved to another city, and the first Catholic parish she found turned out to be "way too liberal for me." She was uncomfortable with the fact that the parish had a Dignity group—for gay and lesbian Catholics. So Frances located a conservative Baptist church that she began to attend.

Intellectually, Frances enjoyed the sermons at the Baptist church. "One thing the Protestants are good at (usually) is giving detailed, Bible-based sermons. I also went to their Sunday school classes." Frances soon realized, however, that she "really missed the Mass. Communion played a very minor role in their services, and I felt that I was going to half a church, because they had a lot of good hymns and the word of God but very little emphasis on the Eucharist."

Frances had learned to speak Russian through her Foreign Service experience, and she wanted someone to practice with. Eventually she located a woman who was a native speaker, and they became good friends. This woman was Russian Orthodox, and Frances became intrigued with that. It "seemed to be just what I was looking for." At this point, Frances thought that the Catholic Church "had the mysticism and the Eucharist but was not biblically based, while the Protestants had the Bible but not the Eucharist. The Orthodox Church seemed to have both, so I began to attend the local Russian Orthodox church."

Frances stayed with this Orthodox parish for about eight years. "They even baptized me, because they claimed that my Catholic baptism was not adequate." Unfortunately, Frances "actually began to feel worse psychologically after meeting up with this Russian lady and getting involved in that church. However, it was a long time before I finally realized that this church was making me sicker and then summoned up the gumption to get out of it. In fact, I had another nervous breakdown in 1994, and that was when I began to figure out what I needed to change in my life."

In the Russian Orthodox parish Frances attended, the requirements for receiving Communion were so strict that most people received it only once or twice a year. "You have to go to the lengthy vespers service on Saturday night, go to Confession, and then fast from midnight Saturday night" to receive Communion on Sunday morning. Frances found these rules too difficult to observe, so she seldom received Communion.

Frances now says that she is "convinced that Holy Communion is medicine from Heaven." In the Catholic Church "most people receive Communion every Sunday, and some people every day. As soon as I returned to Catholicism and began frequent reception of the Blessed Sacrament, I noticed a big change in my health."

After trying a couple of different Catholic parishes, Frances found that the one closest to her home was where she felt she belonged. "Now I have truly found my church home." Frances serves as a lector, and she leads the Sunday Bible study sessions. She is also active in her parish's efforts to encourage evangelization among Catholics.

Frances's final words illustrate how well she understands the connection between the parish and the church as a whole: "I am so thankful to be a Catholic. I love the Mass, and I love the feeling of belonging to a universal church. I deeply regret that I lost so many years away from the church, especially during the papacy of John Paul II, which has been so pivotal for our church. However, perhaps it is better that I did wander away for so many years, because it only helps me to appreciate it more and not take it for granted, as one might be inclined to do otherwise."

Coming home to the Catholic Church cannot be separated from coming home to a specific, less-than-perfect parish. With the pluralism that exists among parishes today, it's important for the returning Catholic to find a parish where he or she feels more or less at home. Still, no matter which parish the returning Catholic identifies with, it is to the one, universal Catholic Church that he or she belongs to.

Returning Catholics do well to resist a consumer attitude toward parishes. Yes, we can try to find the parish where we feel most at home. But once we locate that parish and begin attending Mass there, it's important to not simply sit back and wait for the parish to come to us. Returning Catholics have many gifts to offer, and as we return we should be invited to get involved in parish social, educational, and service-oriented activities. Just as the Mass isn't a spectator activity but one in which all present participate actively, so the membership in a parish community isn't supposed to be passive. Rather, to the extent that the returning Catholic's work and family schedule allows, he or she will get out of parish life what he or she puts into it.

PART TWO

Reaching Out to

Alienated Catholics

The Church Has Obligations

to Alienated Catholics

The spark that ignited Steve's return return to the church after being away for nearly twenty years was a simple billboard message he saw one day that asked: "Are you an inactive or alienated Catholic? We miss you and want you to come home." The billboard gave the phone number of a Catholic parish. Steve thought about it for a few days, then he called.

After the church and Steve reconciled, he was surprised to

find that many of the Catholic parishes in his area did not have the same kind of outreach to inactive Catholics that had brought him back to the church. He was even more perplexed to discover that the diocese in which he lived had no formal outreach program at all.

Every Catholic parish, and every diocese, has an obligation rooted in the Gospel to seek reconciliation with inactive and alienated Catholics. When some 17 million Americans who identify themselves as Catholic also say that they no longer practice the faith, this is no small matter.[1] Indeed, the largest religious group in the United States is made up of inactive Catholics, followed by active Catholics, with Baptists coming in third.[2]

Catholic author Carrie Kemp explains: "We call them alienated, former, lapsed, fallen away, but only rarely do we call them to talk with us, to tell us their stories, to know their goodness and their pain. Unrecognized, the millions who are alienated from our Catholic family become a gaping wound in the Body of Christ—a hemorrhage of anger, frustration, pain, and rejection. Without opportunity for reconciliation and healing, ongoing struggles with the church eventually erode into spiritual deadness, isolation, and hopelessness."[3]

A big part of the problem of institutional Catholic disinterest in reaching out to lapsed or alienated Catholics is that historically the church has rarely thought in terms of a need for such a ministry. Prior to Vatican II, Catholics typically blamed inactive Catholics for moral lapses, and that was the end of the explanation. Inactive or fallen-away Catholics were judged and condemned for being lazy and spiritually blind. It was always entirely the fault of the lapsed Catholic if he or she stayed away from the church. If lapsed Catholics did show up for Mass on Christmas and/or Easter, "good Catholics" looked down their noses at them as if spiritually superior.

Today's parish and diocesan ministers, and Catholics in general, do well to raise serious doubts about this customary perception of lapsed Catholics as morally culpable for being away from the church. Even if a fallen-away Catholic is at fault, to one degree or another, for being an inactive Catholic, ninety-nine times out of a hundred he or she also has a legitimate complaint against the church. Far more often than not, the fallen-away Catholic fell away because the church, either as an institution or in the person of one of its representatives, failed to live up to Gospel ideals. Absolutely essential to the reconciliation process with alienated Catholics is a willingness on the part of parish and diocesan ministers to admit when the church failed and be willing to ask forgiveness for that failure.

This willingness to acknowledge church failures and ask forgiveness for them is the primary obligation that official representatives of the church have with regard to alienated Catholics. Frequently priests, vowed religious, and lay ministers must ask the forgiveness of the alienated Catholic for the church's sin against him or her. A simple question, What would Jesus do? is enough to cut through much of the apparent complexity of an issue and get to the heart of the matter.

It's not so difficult to see that when it comes to alienated Catholics, the real Jesus wants the church to be welcoming, forgiving, and ready to admit church failures, ready to ask forgiveness and be reconciled. Although the details sometimes may be difficult to deal with, the reconciling love of Christ is what it's all about, and there is nothing very complicated about that.

CHAPTER SIX

Successful Outreach Programs for

Alienated Catholics

Catholics involved in parish and diocesan ministries tend to be enthusiastic about "programs." Any predesigned program that promises to meet a specific need is likely to attract considerable attention from these folks. Programs meant to attract alienated Catholics back to the church are no different. As of this writing, most of the efforts to reach out to and be reconciled with Catholics estranged from the church seem to be largely unprogrammatic in nature; they are local, informal, and personal in their orientation. This makes sense, as Catholics have a long history of not being pushy when it comes to dealing with "lapsed" members. This nonassertive philosophy is admirable in some respects, but it can become little more than benevolent apathy. Catholics estranged from the church may even perceive this approach, or lack of approach, to mean that active Catholics feel superior to inactive ones, as if the former don't really care if the latter stay away or not.

It makes perfectly good sense, then, for those responsible for parish and diocesan ministries to take a "program"-oriented approach when it comes to Catholics estranged from the church. Such programs can say to society at large, and to alienated Catholics in particular: "We do indeed care about you, and we hope that we can get together again, because that's the way Christ wants us—together."

The purpose of this chapter is to describe and illustrate the workings of currently available outreach and reconciliation programs for Catholics who are estranged from the church. As noted, many such programs are locally designed, informal, and personal in nature. So to begin we'll look at a more or less typical locally designed and administered program.

ALIENATED CATHOLICS ANONYMOUS

This local program, offered continuously since 1985, owes its existence and success to Monsignor Thomas Cahalane, pastor of Our Mother of Sorrows Parish, in Tucson, Arizona. In the early 1980s, Monsignor Cahalane decided that he wanted to do something about the large number of lapsed Catholics in his area, so he developed Alienated Catholics Anonymous (ACA). An ACA brochure explains that it is "for Catholics exploring reconciliation and return to active participation in their faith."

If alienated Catholics have any contact at all with the church, Monsignor Cahalane realized, quite often it's at Christmas and Easter. These are times when people estranged from the church may be most ready to return. So he schedules his ACA sessions right after these two major holidays, with a third series scheduled in the early fall, after the school year begins. The sessions are scheduled for six consecutive weeks, one evening a week, and the series is facilitated by Monsignor Cahalane, as pastor of the parish, and lay ministers who are members of the parish staff. On its front cover, the ACA brochure quotes the words of Jesus in Matthew 1:29–30: "Come to me, all you who are weary and find life burdensome, and I will refresh you."

Realizing that someone who reads the brochure may be wary and uncertain, this first contact with the program attempts to show the reader that ACA identifies with his or her experience and feelings. The brochure does this by listing a series of possible concerns of alienated Catholics. These include confusion about the church and one's place there; a desire to renew intimacy with God and feel better about oneself; and an interest in getting accurate information about changes in the church in recent decades.

Some potential returnees simply may have come to a time in their lives when they miss active participation in the life of the church, and they may want to learn to pray again and feel closer to God. Others may feel that they have been away from the church for too long. Of course, there are the many whose alienation from the church comes from a divorce and remarriage, and they want to know what they can do to be reconciled with the church.

To reassure those thinking about returning, the brochure explains that each ACA series adapts to the particular needs of each new group. The program also is based on a nonjudgmental acceptance of each person, and it encourages each one to express his or her true feelings and concerns. ACA promises to give a clear understanding of changes in the church since Vatican II. The brochure also offers comments from previous participants on what they liked about the program: "A meeting is very powerful when I do not want it to conclude." "The explanation of the Mass was wonderful." "The informal atmosphere. I felt free to ask questions." "Sitting with mature people and encouraging care for each other."

Monsignor Cahalane explains that Alienated Catholics Anonymous is focused on "creating an environment of hospitality and an invitation for renewal of relationships with Christ and the church."[1] The name of the program, he adds, came from his conviction "that many, many of our Christmas and Easter Catholics are really anonymous because they are not registered with the parish, and for one reason or another they are alienated, too." At the same time, he felt that "many of them are awaiting an opportunity to renew their relationship with the church. They are confused as to where to begin."

A great many people who are estranged from the church, Monsignor Cahalane says, "have the sense of what it means to be Catholic deep within their consciousness. Moreover, they have never been successful at moving away totally from Catholicism." What they're not sure of is how to reconnect and whether the church will welcome them home again. In some cases, in fact, they have tried to reconnect only to be met by legalisms and a refusal to hear them on a personal level.

In cases where alienated Catholics previously have not been able to get someone to listen to their story, they may be especially hesitant about reconciling with the church, after all, they were burned once. They don't want to be burned again. An extra effort to relate to such people on a personal level is particularly important.

The six sessions that make up the Alienated Catholics Anonymous program may be summarized as follows:

Session 1 begins with an expression of welcome and an explanation that the program is designed to be informal and based on the specific questions and concerns of this particular group. The leader—usually the pastor—then asks the group to join him in a prayer—one that will be used at the beginning of each session—that was written by the late American Trappist monk and author Thomas Merton:

> My Lord God, I have no idea where I am going. I do not see the road ahead of me. I cannot know for certain where it will end. Nor do I really know myself, and the fact that I think that I am following Your will does not mean that I am actually doing so. But I believe that the desire to please You does in fact please You, and I hope that I have that desire in all that I am doing. I hope that I will never do anything apart from that desire. And I know that if I do this You will lead me by the right road through I may know nothing about it. Therefore, will I trust You always though I may seem to be lost and in the shadow of death. I will not fear, for You are ever with me, and You will never leave me to face my perils alone.[2]

Following the prayer, the leader gives each person a registration form on which to write name, address, and telephone number. The registration form also includes several open-ended statements about the person's experience and story that he or she is asked to complete:

❋ **"I am here because . . ."**
Some typical responses: "I want to know the changes that the church has gone through in the last ten years."

"I miss being an active part of the church."

"I want to learn to pray again."

"I want to be able to give my son correct answers to his questions about religion."

"I have been away from the church too long."

"I have returned to the sacraments after five years' absence, and I want to get reenforced so that I won't backslide again."

"I feel I have a responsibility to my children, ages four and six, to become involved in the church."

❋ **"My hopes and expectations are . . ."**

Again, some typical responses: "I hope that I can begin to answer some of the many questions I have about the church."

"I hope to understand and clear up some confusion regarding the Catholic religion."

"I hope to be reinstated and feel comfortable even though because of early teaching and divorce I feel excommunicated."

"I want to know more about what the church believes. I converted when I married and feel I may not know all I should."

"I want to return to my roots—the church. I hope to regain the feeling of love I once had for my church. I hope to be able to feel comfortable about my religion again."

❋ **"My fears/apprehensions in being here are . . ."**

Typical responses: "Have I strayed too far?"

"I fear that my questions will not be answered adequately."

"Disappointment if unable to receive the sacraments."

"That the church is not as accepting of multiple marriages as other denominations."

"That I won't live up to the expectations of the church."

❋ **"My feelings about God at this time are . . ."**

Typical responses: "Confused. Don't believe in all that the church believes."

"I go to church and overall I'm happy being in the Catholic Church, but there are a few things I'm not comfortable with."

※ **"The questions/issues I most want answered in these sessions are . . ."**

Again, some typical responses: "Why was the name 'Confession' changed? Why was the Confession procedure changed?"

"Birth control, divorce, homosexuality within the church, and premarital sex."

"Can a back-sliden {sic} Baptist find true happiness in the Catholic Church?"

"Unanointed lay persons handling the Holy Eucharist bugs me and pulls at the threads of my soul."

"Marriage of clergy; infallibility of the pope."

"Is it really okay in God's eyes for me to return and receive the sacraments?"

Once group members complete the registration forms, the pastor shares with the group the story of the Prodigal Son (Luke 15:11–32) and asks if they can identify themselves in some way as a prodigal son or daughter. "Where am I now in relationship to the loving Father?" The pastor explains that the heart and soul of the Catholic Church is healing and reconciliation. In fact, the church has a special welcome-home sacrament called Reconciliation, or Confession.

The pastor concludes the first session by saying that in the next session he will explain in some detail the Sacrament of Reconciliation. He also says that he looks forward to seeing everyone at Mass on Sunday, and if anyone wants to speak with him privately, he would be happy to meet with them. All they need to do is call for an appointment.

Following this first session, the session leader (pastor) also mails each one a personal letter, which reads:

Dear_____

I was delighted to meet you at our Alienated Catholics Anonymous meeting last evening. I know that it is a new and risky venture for you and the others who are searching for new direction and meaning. God's grace works in marvelous ways, and so very, very often I find that out of pain and alienation new and amazing growth develops.

Should you want to contact me personally at any time during these weeks, I want to assure you of the availability of my time, and you may call the parish number. If I am not available when you call, just leave your name and telephone number, and I will be happy to get back to you.

I am just delighted with the participation and response. The response of yourself and the others teaches me so clearly that our church is indeed called to be a reconciling and healing church. Do please pray that the Lord will show us the way to be a healing and reconciling church.

I look forward to seeing you next week and the following weeks at our Wednesday evening sessions.

The theme of the second session is "Coming Home." As he mentioned at the conclusion of the first session, following a group recitation of the Merton prayer, the pastor invites questions on "things Catholic." He responds to any questions the group may have about changes in the way Catholics believe and worship. Then, following a brief coffee break, the group moves into the church for an informal tour.

The pastor shows the group the Reconciliation rooms and explains the differences between these and the old "confessional boxes" of the pre–Vatican II church. He encourages the group to ask any questions about the interior of the church. The pastor also shows the sacristy where the vestments and liturgical implements are stored. It's not unusual for the tour of the church to last for up to an hour and a half, with a great variety of questions coming from the group. The session concludes with a group prayer before the tabernacle where the blessed sacrament is kept.

Session 3 begins once again with the Merton prayer. The theme of this session is human sexuality, including discussions of the place of sexual intimacy in marriage, questions about homosexuality, and the place of celibacy in the church. The pastor also addresses the meaning of Christian marriage, failed marriages and relationships, separation, divorce, and remarriage. He explains the church's annulment procedure and its possibilities as a process for healing and closure. The pastor hands out copies of the official church annulment forms. Anyone who wishes is encouraged to keep the forms and talk with the pastor after the session or during the coming week. Other questions about marriage, divorce, and remarriage are addressed at this time.

During Session 4, following the Merton prayer, the focus is on the centrality of the Mass, or Eucharist, in Catholic life. If possible this session is held in the parish church. The pastor leads the group through the missalette, the booklet left in the pews at all times with all the prayers and readings for the Mass in it.

This session also is used to explain the place of Mary and the saints in Catholicism. Just as Christians pray for one another in this life, so we may ask those now in eternity to pray for us, too. Common questions and misunderstandings related to prayer to the saints are dealt with at this time.

Everyday Catholic customs and practices, including social outreach efforts and the place of Christian service, are the focal point of Session 5. After the group says together the Merton prayer, the pastor explains how the parish is structured, its various committees and organizations, and how to belong and participate fully in the life of the parish community. During this session other members of the parish staff and leaders of parish groups present brief explanations of the various aspects of parish life.

At the conclusion of this session the pastor explains that the next session will be a special celebration of the Mass during which he will explain each part of the Mass before it happens. He also announces that during the coming week, prior to the sixth and final session, he will be available for the celebration of the Sacrament of Reconciliation. Anyone may make a private appointment or come to the church during the regularly scheduled time for this sacrament, on Saturday afternoon.

Session 6, the final session, includes the special celebration of the Eucharist announced at the previous session. Those attending are encouraged to ask questions at any time during the Mass. As the liturgy proceeds, the pastor explains the centrality of the Mass in Catholic tradition, the structure of the ritual from its Passover meal context in Judaism, and an overview of the history of the Mass up to the present.

During the Penitential Rite, early in the Mass, the pastor explains that we always gather as prodigal sons and daughters and petition the Lord to bless us again with his mercy and forgiveness. Prior to the Liturgy of the Word he explains the basic role of the Scriptures in Catholic life and in the Mass, and how we are nourished by the word of God. Following the Prayers of the Faithful the second main part of the Mass occurs, the Liturgy of the Eucharist. The bread and wine are consecrated and become the body and blood of Christ, that is, the whole person of the risen Lord for our spiritual strengthening and healing.

This is followed by the "Prodigal Son's and Daughter's Banquet," which is sponsored by the Former Alienated Catholics Anonymous group, made up of people who returned to the church at earlier times. As the banquet concludes, the pastor invites any of the participants who wish to attend to a specially designated Mass the following Sunday to participate in a simple ritual after the homily or sermon. At that time the pastor will explain to the congregation that anyone who participated in the ACA sessions is now invited to come forward for a brief ceremony of official welcome home. The pastor emphasizes that participation in this brief ritual is entirely voluntary, and returning to the church does not depend on it. The wishes of those who want to remain anonymous are completely respected.

The next Sunday at the Mass designated for this ritual, the pastor invites the ACA participants to join him at the altar. He then gives the entire Eucharistic assembly a brief explanation of the experience the ACA participants have been through and of this welcome-home moment. He then offers a short informal prayer:

Lord, we are a community blessed with your saving, loving presence. We thank you for our brothers and sisters whom you have brought home to us. You have helped us to know through them that we are a healing and reconciling church. Renew them now in faith, hope and love. We ask this through Christ our Lord. Amen.

Then, as the choir sings two verses of "I Will Never Forget You My People," the pastor individually blesses each of the ACA "graduates" and gives each a welcome-home embrace. When the hymn is concluded, the assembly welcomes the group home with applause.

At the end of the ACA sessions, each participant is asked to complete an evaluation form that consists of four open-ended statements. The statements and some sample responses:

"Strengths of the series as I experienced them are . . ."
"Program based on the individual needs of the group. Clear explanations."

"Dialogue between the people before and after sessions and the excellent rapport between the priest and people."

"Clearer understanding of the changes in the church pertaining to Vatican II; a step-by-step explanation of the Mass."

"Nonjudgmental acceptance of people and invitation to them to express feelings."

"Monsignor Tom's attitude of commitment to group; also the use of good humor."

※ **Looking at the series as a whole, what were the three best aspects?**

"The explanation of the Mass was wonderful; the knowledge gained; getting to know each other."

"Trying to squeeze into the charismatic new church with my traditional institutional church with its holy tradition which I miss greatly."

"The informal atmosphere; I felt free to ask questions; Father's ability to explain things."

"There was never the slightest pressure, only encouragement."

※ **Other comments/observations from the sessions?**

"I gained more knowledge in these sessions than I did from four years of Catholic high school."

"The one to one with someone returning was very good. Some of us are shy. I was given this time of great love and peace and forgiveness, and I'm very grateful."

LANDINGS

Another program for alienated Catholics, this one developed on the national level, comes from the Paulist Fathers. Called "Landings," this program's introductory materials describe it thus: "A Soft Place: Program for Returning Catholics offers a safe place for them to land."

Helen Osman, a reporter for the *Catholic Spirit,* the official Catholic newspaper for the Diocese of Austin, Texas, wrote an article about Landings based on an interview with Paulist Father Jac Campbell, who began the program in 1989.[3] Osman began by pointing out—as we have already seen—that the Catholic Church is the single largest religious group in the United States. At the same time, "it has the dubious distinction of being related to the second-largest religious group in this country: the 20 million inactive Catholics who no longer attend Mass or are involved in parish life."

Like Alienated Catholics Anonymous, Landings is an attempt to reach out to and bring back home to the church the millions of alienated and inactive Catholics who have little or no contact with the church. Although the program has a national base with the Paulist Fathers, it is designed for use on the local parish level. Father Campbell wanted to keep the program simple, so he based it on a simple invitation to Catholics interested in returning to the practice of their faith. These people are invited to join a group of active members of a parish for six to eight evening sessions. The members of the parish, rather than a priest, lead the two-hour sessions, each of which follows a predesigned format.

The idea behind Landings is not to dump a load of abstract theology on a group of alienated Catholics. Rather, a group of trained Catholic laypeople share their own faith journeys in an open and constructive manner. By doing this they encourage potential returnees to the church to do something similar—to talk about their own experience, ask questions, and deal with their own unique faith-related issues.

Marian was attracted back to the church by hearing other

people talk about their struggles with faith. "Even the 'good Catholics'—the ones who had stayed—had struggles with their faith," she commented. "I didn't feel like I was the only one learning." Marian had stopped attending Mass even before she divorced an abusive husband, and she felt stigmatized by both of her choices. "I just felt that I didn't belong in the church," she explained, "and Landings helped take the guilt away from me.

"In the past," Marian continued, "I think the church made you feel guilty about your feelings." This has not been her experience since returning to the church. She tells people estranged from the church not to be afraid of it, as she finds the church a safe place to be, especially the parish she now belongs to. "The community is so loving. They care about people and worry about your sins later."

Basic to Landings is a readiness on the part of both professional parish ministers and ordinary parish members to listen to and respect the faith stories of returning Catholics. Hearing ordinary Catholics talk about their difficulties with the church and some of the church's teachings helps returning Catholics, or those thinking about returning, to deal with their own difficulties.

Mike felt welcomed into the church after he decided to confront his own alcoholism. After his father began recovery from alcoholism through Alcoholics Anonymous, Mike said he knew that his own recovery would be a spiritual path. He decided to turn to the church instead of looking to AA or other self-help programs. Mike said that Landings was "a wonderful experience. It really was a soft landing to come back to the church." The sense of community and spiritual camaraderie Mike found with others in his Landings group led him to seek spiritual direction, which he found quite helpful. Later, after the Landings sessions ended, he and some other members of the group continued their meetings by getting together to discuss a book they all read.

Father Jac Campbell wrote a preamble for the Landings program, which includes the following:

Welcome to the beginning of your Landings journey. Hopefully, you will find here the help, peace and enjoyment thousands of others have found in Landings.

Landings is a uniquely contemporary approach to reconciliation ministry. Landings gives someone who is considering returning an insight into the actual faith lives of a few other Catholics. Landings is not a discussion group. Landings is not a class. It is an experience of faith sharing.

More than anything else Landings is a ministry of compassionate listening. Some call listening the language of God. Over the course of the weeks each person, the welcoming Catholic and the returnee, will have ample and equal opportunity to both speak and be heard.

Few of us are listened to enough, so we may not know how to limit ourselves when we encounter a receptive audience. The timekeeper plays an important role in helping the group maintain the necessary limits, so that everyone can be heard.

Welcoming members are part of the faith-sharing process and are not here to cure, teach, "fix," or in any way to sit in judgment of anyone else's opinions or faith stance. Compassionate listening works best when there is no interrupting, arguing, questioning one another or commenting on what another said.

If you respect the guidelines, enough of your Catholic identity will emerge to provide returning members with a genuine, balanced look into the mind and heart of the Catholic faith as it is lived and expressed in your parish.

Those who feel comfortable returning to Communion with the Church discover during the process that they are just as holy, just as smart, just as beloved by God, just as Catholic, as the rest of us. . . .

The preamble concludes by emphasizing that the program is characterized by confidentiality and trust, by explaining that a resource person will always be available for discussions outside of formal meeting times, by a reminder that those who administer the program should stick to the guidelines, and by an acknowledgment that each person's spiritual journey is sacred and should be respected as such. Finally, the preamble expresses confidence that those who participate can expect to grow in faith and understanding through the Landings program.[4]

A Landings document titled "Founded on Mercy" places the program within the context of the parable of the Prodigal Son, explaining that "the foundation of all Christian life [is] the mercy of God."[5] This document also places Landings within the context of a post–Vatican II, renewed understanding of the Sacrament of Reconciliation and within the Paulist Fathers' long tradition of reconciliation. It concludes by quoting the bishops of the United States: "We want to let our inactive brothers and sisters know that they always have a place in the Church and that we are hurt by their absence—as they are. We want to show our regret for any misunderstandings or mistreatments. And we want to help them see that, however they feel about the Church, we want to talk with them, share with them and accept them as brothers and sisters."[6]

ONCECATHOLIC: AN INTERNET SERVICE FOR RETURNING CATHOLICS

Finally there is an Internet program sponsored by the Franciscan Friars and their magazine, *St. Anthony Messenger.* It's called

OnceCatholic, and its purpose is to help inactive and alienated Catholics reconnect to a local Catholic faith community. The Internet address for this program is *www.oncecatholic.org.* This website offers information and opportunities for interaction with others, personal responses, and referral to coming-home programs within the Catholic Church in the United States.

Eight chat rooms offer a connection that is both "cyber" and personal with a "companion" who is a pastoral minister in the church. The themes for the eight areas are: "Marriage Issues," "Not Being Fed Spiritually," "Just Drifted Away," "Quarrel with a Church Representative," "Feeling Excluded from the Church," "Abortion and/or Post-Abortion Issues," and "Difficulty with a Church Teaching." A general area also exists, where those who don't think they fit into any of the other chat rooms can go to discuss their own story or issue. OnceCatholic has the official support of Bishop Daniel Pilarczyk, of the Diocese of Cincinnati, Ohio, where the program originates.

OnceCatholic is an Internet resource that gives inactive and returning Catholics an easy, no-risk way to make an initial contact with the church and get answers to questions from reliable sources. Ultimately, the goal of OnceCatholic is to put people in touch with someone in their local area who can provide a direct, personal contact with the church.

All of the programs for alienated and returning Catholics have the same purpose: to bring about reconciliation between inactive and/or estranged Catholics and the church. Although the details may differ between the various programs, whether local or national in origin, they all express the Catholic Church's basic desire to invite alienated Catholics to come home and to facilitate that homecoming experience.

Each Catholic parish has unique characteristics, of course. There are rural, suburban, and urban parishes, large and small parishes, parishes with a great many young families and those with a large retired population. Each parish's outreach efforts for alienated Catholics need to take into account not only its own unique characteristics but those of the large population from which it will attract alienated Catholics.

A parish located in a medium-size city with a large state university population, for example, is likely to find itself serving young adults who have not been away from the church for a great many years but are returning after some years of simple adolescent uncertainty about religion and the church. A large urban parish, on the other hand, is more likely to find itself attracting people with a history of many years away from the church. Regardless, a parish welcome-home program needs to be, above all, a program based on sympathetic listening and a readiness to both forgive and ask forgiveness. Everything else is almost incidental.

CHAPTER SEVEN

When Engaged Couples Are Uncertain

About the Church

Marla and Richard are typical of many young engaged couples who approach Catholic parishes today with marriage in mind. Richard grew up in a Catholic family, while Marla grew up in a religiously indifferent family. At age twenty-four, however, Richard has not been inside a Catholic church since he was in high school. The fact is that Richard is about as indifferent toward religion as Marla, but now that they have decided to marry, Richard's Catholic roots have led them to a Catholic parish.

Like many young couples in the first decade of the twenty-first century, Richard and Marla are cohabiting, in their case a choice they made two years ago. Like many in their generation, they have never seen a necessary connection between sex and marriage. For them, sex is a special way to express their affection for each other, but it doesn't necessarily mean a couple must be married. They are genuinely mystified when older adults disapprove of their behavior.

Marla agreed that she would be willing to have a Catholic wedding, but she has no interest in becoming a Catholic. Richard wants a Catholic wedding simply because that's how he was raised, even though he has no current interest becoming an observant, practicing Catholic. He thinks of himself as Catholic only in terms of how he grew up, not in terms of his present or future life. He sees no necessary connection between having a Catholic wedding and being a "practicing Catholic." At the same time, he would be offended if he and Marla were told by a priest or another representative of the church that they could not have a Catholic wedding if they had no intention to live a Catholic life.

Richard is intuitively aware, however, that he will be questioned about his current status as a Catholic if he and Marla approach his parents' pastor about their wedding. So he asks his mother to broach the subject with the pastor—"to run interference for us," as Richard puts it. Richard's mother agrees because she would like her son to have a Catholic wedding.

Fortunately for Richard, Marla, and Richard's parents, the priest Richard's mother talks with is understanding and not inclined to take a legalistic approach to the situation. With no firm basis in church rules, some priests are inclined to insist on the absolute ideal—that a couple must be attending Mass every Sunday at the very least—before they will agree to preside at a church wedding for them.

In a parish where there is a sensitivity to inviting inactive and/or alienated Catholics back to the church, couples such as Richard and Marla will be greeted with hospitality, patience, tolerance, and the love of Christ. A thorough examination of relevant church documents reveals that there is, in fact, no official church support for priests and others who would deny a "nonpracticing" engaged couple a Catholic wedding.[1]

If a young man and woman agree that they want a Catholic wedding, if at least one of them is a baptized Catholic, and if they encounter resistance from a priest, deacon, or parish lay minister because they admit to not attending Mass every Sunday—or even rarely—the couple should know that they have other options. They can contact the local bishop and lodge a complaint, and they also can look for another parish, where they will receive a warmer welcome. The point is that no engaged couple of goodwill—meaning a couple that shows no overt antagonism toward the church—can be denied a church wedding on the basis of nonregular Mass attendance alone.

That said, it is important for all persons concerned to understand that parish priests, deacons, and lay ministers do have an obligation to provide engaged couples with adequate marriage preparation. This preparation may take various forms, but it should include opportunities for the couple to examine their relationship in depth and catechesis on Catholic beliefs concerning marriage. In the case of cohabiting couples, marriage preparation also should include an honest look at the real long-range risks of premarital cohabitation based on scientific research that has been done on couples who cohabited prior to marriage.[2]

Priests, deacons, and lay ministers responsible for ministry to engaged couples are well advised to formulate specific diocesan and parish policies regarding how nonpracticing engaged couples are to be received by parishes. There are two options. The first option is to verbally stiff-arm the couple by telling them to get their Catholic act together and start attending Mass every Sunday, then come back to talk about the wedding. This option is virtually guaranteed to increase the couple's alienation from the church and perhaps guarantee that the young man and woman will never darken the door of a Catholic church again. If we ask the question "What would Jesus do?" it is impossible to imagine the Jesus we find in the Gospels doing anything like this.

Close examination of the Jesus presented to us by the Gospels of Matthew, Mark, Luke, and John shows us a Jesus who is a minimalist when it comes to rules and regulations of all kinds. In the Gospel of Mark, for example, Jesus declares: "The sabbath was made for humankind, and not humankind for the sabbath . . ." (2:27). In other words, traditions and laws exist to serve people; people do not exist to serve traditions and laws.

Couples not attending Mass regularly who approach a parish about scheduling a Catholic wedding should be welcomed as Christ would—and does—welcome them: with open arms, warmth, and joy. In the context of this welcome, such couples need also to be challenged to grow deeper in their love for each other. At the same time, it is important that the priest or deacon not immediately confront the marginally Catholic couple with questions about faith and religion that they may perceive as threatening.

Father Joseph M. Champlin, a parish priest in the Diocese of Syracuse, New York, for over forty years, offers a good example in the ways he routinely deals with couples whose connections to the church are marginal, at best.[3] Father Champlin first makes sure that his first significant contact with the couple is a personal meeting, not a phone call. Typically, couples are both excited about getting married and nervous and apprehensive about making contact with "the church." As long as the initial telephone contact communicates to the couple that the parish, and the priest or deacon in particular, is looking forward to meeting them, then the couple's anxiety will be decreased significantly by the time they arrive for their first in-person meeting.

During the couple's first meeting with him, Father Champlin asks a series of nonthreatening questions to establish a comfortable and trusting interaction. These questions are:

※ "Where do you work?" Almost anyone is comfortable talking about his or her work, so this gets the conversation off on the right foot and serves as a kind of "icebreaker."

※ "How did you meet?" Couples enjoy telling the story of how they met and got to know each other. Sometimes these stories are humorous, and sometimes they reveal something important about the couple that may be used later in the marriage preparation process to help them deal with a significant issue prior to their wedding.

※ "What was your first impression of each other?" In some cases, the future spouses have never told each other this, so the question not only continues the "icebreaker" phase but may reveal still more about the couple's relationship that may be used as discussion material later on.

※ "Why do you think you fell in love with each other?" At this point the discussion gets rather "heavy," as it is unlikely that the couple has ever talked about this question. They may even find themselves stammering and uncertain about how to respond. Instead of simply letting the couple sit there and squirm, however, the priest or deacon might offer some helpful comments, such as a remark that falling in love is a deeply complex process and even in-depth psychological analysis might find it difficult to come up with reasons we fall in love with a particular person. Some psychological theories suggest that a person tends to fall in love with someone who balances or complements him or her emotionally and psychologically. For example, someone who is quiet and reserved might fall in love with someone who is outgoing and who finds it easy and enjoyable to meet new people and talk with them. These comments help to draw out the couple and lead them into what may actually become a profound discussion about their own relationship.

※ "What do you each find to be the most endearing quality in the other?" The purpose of this question is to further encourage "positive vibes" between the couple and the priest or deacon who is conducting the interview. The young man and woman may blush a bit as they say what they like most about each other, but that's fine. This question gives the priest or deacon a chance to show some appreciation for the couple and for their love for each other. Before addressing any difficult issues such as a marriage between partners with different religious backgrounds, marginal participation in church life, or the fact that this may be a second marriage for one or both of the partners, this is a moment for the couple and the priest or deacon to "bask" in the couple's love for each other.

Most parish ministers responsible for marriage preparation today make use of helpful relationship surveys to stimulate constructive discussion and to gauge in an objective manner the couple's preparedness for marriage. Three such surveys are used most often in the United States today:

1. *PMI (Pre-Marital Inventory) Profile.* Available from Intercommunication Publishing, Inc., 1 Valentine Lane, Chapel Hill, NC 27514.

2. FOCCUS (Facilitating Open Couple Communication, Understanding, and Study). Prepared by the Archdiocese of Omaha, 1984. FOCCUS, Family Life Office, 3214 N. 60th Street, Omaha, NE 68104.

3. PREPARE-ENRICH (Premarital Personal and Relationship Enrichment). Available from Prepare-Enrich, Inc., P.O. Box 190, Minneapolis, MN 55440.

It's vitally important to emphasize with the engaged couple that such inventories are *not* a "test" to determine whether they may marry or not. Rather, they are simply instruments that are helpful to bring up issues of potential conflict in the couple's relationship that need to be discussed. The purpose of any of these inventories is to spark discussion and good communication, period.

It is also important for any engaged couple, but especially for a couple that includes one or more inactive Catholics, that a formal marriage preparation program be a part of the months leading up to their wedding. Most young couples—and particularly older couples—can see the value of such programs and are happy to participate for the sake of their future marriage. Indeed, it's a sign of maturity in a couple if they are enthusiastic about participation in whatever marriage preparation opportunities are offered them.

In the United States, four kinds of marriage preparation programs are available for couples planning Catholic weddings: (1) private sessions with a professional counselor; (2) locally sponsored group programs; (3) Engaged Encounter; and (4) sponsor couple programs. Some couples may participate in two or more of these programs, but most attend only one in addition to their meetings with the priest or deacon who is the primary person responsible for helping them to prepare for marriage.

Professional Counseling

Sessions with a professional counselor vary in number and content, but typically the counselor tries to help the couple understand themselves and each other better in terms of their earlier family and other experiences. He or she also tries to help the couple learn some basic communication and conflict resolution skills. One big advantage of professional counseling is the individualized attention the engaged couple receives. One drawback is that the couple has no opportunity to get a variety of perspectives from both married and engaged couples in a formal marriage preparation setting.

Local Group Marriage Preparation Programs

Locally sponsored group marriage preparation programs may consist of a series of evening or one-day sessions—for example, on three consecutive Saturdays—attended by a group of engaged couples. Or the program may have a weekend format where the group of engaged couples stay at a retreat facility from Friday evening through early Sunday afternoon. Regardless of the format, the content typically consists of presentations by married couples, and often a priest, on topics relating to marriage, such as communication, sexuality, conflict resolution, marriage as a sacrament, and some basic parenting skills. Frequently these presentations are followed by opportunities for the couples to discuss the topic just covered, often utilizing forms each one fills out and discusses with his or her future spouse. Quite often these group programs also include opportunities for the engaged couples to interact with the other couples and gain perspective from each others thoughts and experiences.

Engaged Encounter

Engaged Encounter is a program that developed as an offshoot of the Worldwide Marriage Encounter organization. This international program is highly structured so that presentations given by married couples and a priest—almost always veterans of Marriage Encounter—must fit into a predesigned outline that remains the same for all Engaged Encounter groups. The married couples and priest give presentations on various topics related to marriage, and after each presentation the engaged couples receive a set of questions. The future spouses separate from each other and write responses to these questions, then the two get back together and discuss what they wrote. This format is virtually identical to the format used by Marriage Encounter, but the topics are geared to engaged rather than married couples. As far as marginally Catholic engaged couples are concerned, the Engaged Encounter experience can be a moment when the faith of the married couples and the priest can touch their lives in positive ways.

Sponsor Couple Programs

Sponsor couple program resources are available from various publishers of catechetical materials, but the format is similar regardless of the specific program materials used. Typically, a local parish priest, deacon, or lay minister matches the engaged couple with a veteran married couple to serve as a "mentor couple" for the couple preparing for marriage. The engaged couple meets several times with the married couple, usually in the latter's home, to discuss various topics related to marriage and to share their experience of married life.

In a sponsor couple program, the engaged couple receives considerable individualized attention, which is a big plus. At the same time, a sponsor couple program has the advantage of giving the married couple many opportunities to share with the engaged couple on a faith level. If the engaged couple includes one or two people whose Catholic connections are tenuous, through their care and concern the married couple can help the engaged couple to feel the welcoming love of Christ for them. The point is not, of course, for the married couple to pressure the engaged couple to conform to rigid expectations about participation in church life. Rather, by their witness to the impact of Christ's loving presence in their marriage over the years, the married couple may have a positive impact on the engaged couple, if not in the short run then maybe in the long run.

THE MEANING OF
A CATHOLIC WEDDING

Regardless of the program in which the engaged couple participates, if the engaged man and woman are in a distanced relationship to the church, the marriage preparation process is a time when they can be helped to see that marriage in the church is a sacrament. The man and woman are the ministers of the sacrament of marriage, not the priest, who serves as a witness on behalf of the church. Therefore, at least a minimal faith stance is necessary on the part of the couple for a wedding to be celebrated in a Catholic church.

It is never the responsibility of the active Catholics involved

in presenting or administering marriage preparation programs
to evaluate or judge the faith of an engaged couple. But they
can, and should, help the couple to discern their position honestly, and ultimately it is the responsibility of the priest who
will witness the couple's marriage to confirm that at least one of
the two engaged persons has at least a minimal level of Catholic
faith. Even if this is only the seedling of faith, it still may be suf-
ficient for an engaged couple to celebrate a Catholic wedding,
and ultimately they should be given the benefit of the doubt.
This seems to be what Christ would do, and this is what the
church's official representatives should strive to do as well.

In fact, the priest, deacon, or lay minister who works with
the engaged couple should help them to decide whether it is appropriate for them to have a Catholic wedding or not. The
church's representative should never deliver a judgment on
whether the couple has "enough faith" to have a Catholic wedding. In the end, the choice should be the couple's. As long as
either the man or woman is a baptized Catholic and chooses to
have a Catholic wedding, the church's official representatives do
well to cooperate, as long as they help the couple, to the best of
their ability, to understand that a Catholic wedding is meant to
celebrate not just a wedding but the beginning of a marriage
based on and rooted in a life lived in union with the risen Christ.

READINESS FOR MARRIAGE

With any engaged couple, but especially in the case of a couple
that includes at least one person who has been away from the
church, it is vitally important for parish ministers, both clergy
and laity, to help the two people come to a clear vision of their
readiness for marriage. In a popular culture where it can be easy

to mistake infatuation or an unrealistically romantic outlook for the kind of love that will keep a marriage alive for fifty or sixty years, parish ministers must help engaged couples to clarify their perspective on each other and on their commitment to marriage. The high percentage of marriages that end in divorce should give any couple pause, and this is the time to take advantage of that pause. All concerned should take seriously the statistical fact, for example, that among couples who have a shared religious faith, the divorce rate is about half that of the general population.

The limitations on the ability of anyone to gauge a couple's readiness for marriage are extreme, to be sure. No one has a crystal ball into which to gaze to see whether a given couple's marriage will last "until death do us part" or end up as wreckage on the shoals of life. More than a few marriages that looked iffy in the extreme at the beginning ended up lasting a lifetime, and more than a few marriages that looked ideal at the start have ended in a painful divorce. So who can say? All the same, the church's ministers, priests, deacons, and laity have a responsibility to do all they can to help each engaged couple take a good long look at themselves and each other and ask the hard questions.

In the case of couples that include at least one inactive or estranged Catholic, this process of self-examination should, in the context of a warm welcome, include the encouragement to ask about the reasons for wanting to have a Catholic wedding. One frequent reason has to do with wanting to please parents and extended family. But the couple should be encouraged to ask if this is truly reason enough to have a Catholic wedding. If the couple feels that it is, then a priest, deacon, or lay minister would do well to not throw up roadblocks. This is, after all, a moment when the couple may either leave the door open to a future return to full participation in the life of the church or close the door forever. Again, the question the church's representatives need to ask in such a situation is "What would Jesus do?" It's difficult to imagine that the Jesus we find in the Gospels would do anything but leave the door wide open for a future return. As long as at least one of the engaged partners is a baptized Catholic, there is no room for any other action on the part of the church's representatives.

USE THE WEDDING PLANNING TIME FOR MORE THAN THAT

It's true that marriage preparation offered by the church is primarily about preparing for marriage, not preparing for the wedding. Still, at some point it becomes appropriate for the couple to begin planning for their wedding, too. During the marriage preparation process ideally the couple comes to a deeper appreciation for the fact that the wedding and reception are over in a few hours and what they are left with is a marriage meant to go on for a lifetime. All the same, most couples understandably want a beautiful, memorable wedding.

In many cases today the person who helps the couple plan their wedding will be someone other than the priest who will preside at their wedding. The couple must recognize that the wedding liturgy, whether in the context of a Mass or not, *is* explicitly Catholic in all of its aspects. It can be particularly helpful for the wedding planner to help an engaged couple who has been on the church's margins to see the connections between their wedding and their faith, rudimentary as it may be.

The wedding liturgy contains three readings and a responsorial psalm. The engaged couple must choose from among several options for each reading. To do so, the couple must, at the very least, read through the options and decide which they think fits them best. They also need to decide who will do the first two readings and the responsorial psalm; the final reading is the Gospel, which the priest or deacon reads.

The couple also must choose among several options for the exchange of wedding vows, and they may choose to recite together a brief set of prayers following the exchange of vows. If the wedding is to be in the context of a Mass, choices also need to be made about the content of the Prayer of the Faithful and who will lead that prayer. The couple also chooses which Prayer Over the Gifts they want the priest to say.

Whether the wedding includes a Mass or not, the couple chooses which Nuptial Blessing they want the priest or deacon to pray over them, which Prayer After Communion they want the priest to recite, and from among several formulas for the Final Blessing.

Add to this the sacred music the couple wants to include in their wedding, and whether they want to include the ritual of lighting a wedding candle to symbolize the ideal of two in one, and it is evident that they have more than enough choices to keep them busy with the wedding alone.

Each and every one of these choices requires the engaged couple to come to a decision in the light of their faith—again, regardless of how rudimentary it may be. Therefore, the process of planning the wedding can itself be a time for the couple to ponder the place of Christian faith and the Catholic Church in their future as a married couple. The person who helps the couple to plan the wedding, if he or she is wise and sensitive, will gently encourage them to be guided by their faith to make choices that truly reflect their deepest spiritual ideals.

Charles and Krista were married five years ago, and today they describe themselves as being "brought back to the church by the caring, kindness, and understanding" of the priest responsible for their marriage preparation process and the woman on the parish staff who helped them plan their wedding. Krista explains that they didn't immediately become "full-time, active Catholics." In fact, after their wedding they soon slipped back into their prewedding habit of not having much to do with the church.

Two years later, however, Krista was pregnant with the couple's first child, and they began to think about wanting to be the kind of people they wanted to be as parents. "We talked about it several times over the course of a couple of months or so," Charles recalls, "and basically what it came down to was that we decided that we should start acting like adults, and for both of us that included being active Catholics, going to Mass on Sundays, participating in parish activities, that sort of thing."

Krista had not been a Catholic when the couple met and married, but she had been touched by the warm reception she and Charles received when they approached a Catholic parish about being married in the church. During Krista's growing-up years her family had belonged to a mainline Protestant church, but by the time she was a teenager Krista had become "turned off" by the heavy emphasis on the "reading the Bible and looking for answers there to everything that came up." During the couple's marriage preparation process, on the other hand, Krista had been delighted with what struck her as the Catholic Church's "balanced use of the Bible, not as if it's the be-all and the end-all, but in the context of the Mass and in the context of finding God in all kinds of other places too, not only in the Bible."

Krista and Charles had moved away from the city and parish where they were married, but they went looking for a Catholic parish where they now live, and Krista participated in the Rite of Christian Initiation for Adults with Charles as her sponsor. "I think I learned about as much as Krista did," Charles comments.

"It really gave us both a better understanding of the Catholic Church and what it means to live as a Catholic in today's world. We don't agree with absolutely everything that goes on in the church—I don't think most Catholics do—but we feel very much at home in the church, and we want to share that with our children, both here in our own home and in our parish."

Clearly, if Charles and Krista had not had a good experience with the church as an engaged couple, they might never have returned to the church later on. This determination to offer marginally Catholic engaged couples a blend of warm welcome and challenge to be honest with each other and the church about their relationship with the church constitutes the best form of what we might call "remote preparation" for a permanent return to the church. By taking this approach, a parish says to the engaged couple, "We know who we are as a church, and we want nothing but the best for you. Since at least one of you is a baptized Catholic, we welcome you for your wedding, and we invite you to decide for yourselves if your reasons for marrying in the church coincide with the church's understanding of marriage. We don't ask you to be perfect, and we hope you won't expect us to be perfect, either. We hope that one day you will want to participate fully in the life of the church."

Many parish priests and lay ministers understand the connection between marriage and active involvement in the life of a parish. They know that in the life of a married couple, the marriage itself is the primary "place" where the couple encounters God's loving grace. The marriage itself is the source of the couple's most basic religious experiences, the place where they most commonly encounter God. Many other parish priests and lay ministers do *not* have a firm grasp of this truth and of its implications. But one of the primary implications of this insight is that an excellent way to nurture the faith of a married couple, or touch the couple on the level of faith, is to show an interest in supporting their marriage and family life.

One of the best ways for a parish to reach out to inactive and alienated Catholics is to make the support of marriage and family life a major parish priority and get the word out about this in as many ways as possible.

CHAPTER EIGHT

When Adult Offspring Are Alienated

from the Church

When young people who are teenagers and in their early twenties refuse to attend Mass, it's fairly easy for parents to chalk it up to normal adolescent rebellion or a need to question and establish one's own values and identity. It's quite another matter when young-adult offspring seem to make a final decision to distance themselves from the church. This can be a source of tremendous heartache for parents who did all they could during the child's growing-up years to pass along to him or her the Catholic faith. The fact that children of friends grow up to be mature, dedicated Catholics only seems to pour salt on the wound. It's only natural for parents to ask themselves "What did we do wrong?"

The answer to this question is almost always "Nothing." No parents get perfect kids, of course, and no kids get perfect parents, so it's futile to wonder, in retrospect, "Where did we go wrong?" because there will ever be ways parents could have raised their children differently. The truth is that almost all parents do the best they can, and that's all they should expect of themselves. Yes, it's easy for parents whose children embrace the Catholic faith for themselves to breathe a sigh of relief. But all they did was they best they could do. It's all a big mystery, and the story is ongoing, whether adult children have chosen to be Catholic or have chosen to not be Catholic. Those who chose Catholicism could still change their minds, and those who are estranged could still return.

Veteran pastor and author Father Joseph Champlin offers the following observations: Certain events usually characterize the movement of young adults away from their Catholic roots. "They stop going regularly to Sunday Mass, they move in with their significant other; they marry out of the church; they fail to have their own children baptized."

This wandering away from the church naturally causes Catholic parents more than a little heartache. But Father Champlin offers the following thoughts that may provide some comfort and could even help lead to the return of adult offspring to the church.[1]

Most parents I know keep asking themselves, "Where did we fail?" What did we do wrong?" when their young daughter becomes pregnant without a wedding ring or their youthful son succumbs to some serious addiction. They torture themselves with similar questions when offspring neglect or abandon their Catholic traditions.

For most situations, parents took their upbringing tasks seriously. They were responsible tutors and modeled their religious teaching by active practice.

No one is perfect, however, Father Champlin continues. All parents have their flaws, so no parenting has been mistake free. At the same time, parents cannot take upon themselves full responsibility for the bad choices and inappropriate behavior of their children.

We give them roots and wings; we point out the way; we provide good examples and correct when necessary. God bestows the precious gift of freedom upon human beings and thus allows us to choose virtue or vice, make good or bad choices. Parents in somewhat similar fashion can only step back and with worry or perhaps disappointment watch their young adult children make decisions contrary to what they had been taught.

Blaming themselves causes parents to bear a false and irrational guilt, which, while painful, does not really require God's forgiveness, but rather inner healing based upon a better appreciation of the limited role they have in raising children. Worry? Understandable. Self-blame or guilt? Irrational and not helpful.

It can be helpful to be aware of current trends and statistics, Father Champlin says. It's good for parents to view their own experience in a bigger context, one that reveals something of the bigger picture.

Current surveys indicate that a majority of young Catholics attend Mass each weekend until they reach eighteen, then the figure drops to about 32 percent. The graph does not upturn until these young adults pass the age of twenty-eight.

There are no precise times for a conversion of heart or return to the church. Nevertheless, marriage and baptism may trigger some stirring of faith within the inactive Catholic. Moreover, we do experience a significant number of "returns" with the First Communion of the first child, especially when a parish provides or requires active involvement of the parents in the preparation process for that sacrament. In addition, the death of someone close or [a major tragedy] . . . frequently can lead a raised but dormant Catholic back to his or her roots. An awareness of these trends should bring comfort and encouragement to dedicated Catholic parents.

Father Champlin also emphasizes that parents do well to make their own feelings clear when young adults seem to sever their ties with the church:

During the early stages of their children slipping away from the church, parents at one point need to express very clearly to their offspring that these departures from practicing the faith cause them great sadness. The young adults need to know that their actions or nonactions bring pain to the parents. The children probably sense that, but should hear this explicitly articulated.

But after that, no nagging; no constantly getting on their cases. Instead, prayers, good example and unconditional love are in order. God's love for us is constant and does not cease when our own behavior fails to follow divine directives. Parents' love for their children should seek to imitate that unceasing care and love.

Father Champlin concludes with the observation that when God's grace—his gift of his very self to us—does gently nudge the young-adult children in the direction of returning to their Catholic spiritual roots, this always-welcoming parental love will make that homecoming much easier to accomplish.

David M. Thomas, a veteran spouse and parent as well as a theologian and authority on family ministry, comes at this issue from unique but complementary directions. He suggests that parents consider that their young-adult child may simply be "going through a necessary time of reevaluation." He or she may be asking "Is what I accepted on my parents' authority the best for me? Maybe yes, maybe no. But to evaluate it, I must step back and think about who I am and what I stand for."

The goal of our faith, Thomas continues, is that "our response to God be adult—that means that it must be our own and not borrowed from the faith of another."

David Thomas also invites parents to look at the adult offspring's total life picture. "Is there basic goodness, concern for others, dedication to values? We all go through phases in our lives. It's like the space between stepping-stones. For an instant we lose touch with one stone before we land on another. In the time in between, we must think and examine what's next."[2]

It's important for the parents of young adults who distance themselves from the church to realize that, in the long run, their children are God's children more than they are the children of their human parents. Parents need to place their ultimate trust in God's love and trust that the One whom Jesus made it a major point to call "Father" will never abandon their children, no matter what. They remain in their loving Father's care regardless, for God's love is, in fact, bigger than the church.

Such trust doesn't come easily, of course, and parents may find themselves tempted to despair of being able to influence their grown offspring at all. It's practically trite to whistle up the memory of Saint Monica, the mother of Saint Augustine of Hippo (354–430) who became one of the early church's greatest theologians and a doctor of the church. Early in his life, Augustine gave his mother reasons to despair that any modern parent can identify with. Monica was a Christian, but Augustine ignored her good example and joined the Manichaean cult. He lived with a woman to whom he was not married, and she gave birth to a son, Adeodatus. For some twenty years Monica prayed persistently that Augustine might be converted to Christianity, and only after all that time and in the midst of a spiritual crisis did he embrace the faith. In his famous *Confessions,* speaking to God, Augustine wrote about Monica that "in the flesh she brought me to birth in this world: in her heart she brought me to birth in your eternal life."

There was a time when priests and teachers always recommended to the parents of fallen-away children that they ask Saint Monica to pray for their children's return to the church. This remains good advice today. Sometimes parents don't have enough confidence in the power of prayer to bring others—including their own adult children who are estranged from the church—back to the practice of the faith. The truth is that we don't completely understand how prayers of petition "work." We can't say that only if we beg and plead for years and years is it possible that God may finally relent and come across with what we ask for. This would imply a God who doesn't care about the anguish of parents. Rather, it is the adult child who needs our patience. At the same time, there is no ignoring one of Jesus' best-known stories:

> And he said to them, "Suppose one of you has a friend, and you go to him at midnight and say to him, 'Friend, lend me three loaves of bread; for a friend of mine has arrived, and I have nothing to set before him.' And he answers from within, 'Do not bother me; the door has already been locked,

and my children are with me in bed; I cannot get up and give you anything.' I tell you, even though he will not get up and give him anything because he is his friend, at least because of his persistence he will get up and give him whatever he needs.

"So I say to you, Ask, and it will be given you; search, and you will find; knock, and the door will be opened for you." (Luke 11:5–9)

With this story Jesus encourages persistence in petitionary prayer, prayer that asks God for specifics. There is nothing vague about what the petitioner in this story wants, and it seems clear that by telling this story Jesus approves for his followers the practice of asking God for exactly what we want and need. So parents of wandering adult offspring should feel perfectly okay about asking God to give their children the grace to return to the practice of the Catholic faith. At the same time, we need to take note of the verses that follow the ones just quoted. These verses start off in a clear and encouraging manner, but then Jesus' words take a perplexing turn:

"For everyone who asks receives, and everyone who searches finds, and for everyone who knocks, the door will be opened.

"Is there anyone among you who, if your child asks for a fish, will give a snake instead of a fish? Or if the child asks for an egg, will give a scorpion? If you then, who are evil, know how to give good gifts to your children, how much more will the heavenly Father give the Holy Spirit to those who ask him!" (Luke 11:10–13)

Luke's Jesus assures his listeners that persistence in asking will receive a positive response. If you ask you will receive; if you search you will find; and if you knock the door will open. If we, who often don't have our heads screwed on straight, know what it means to give good things to our children, we need have no doubt that our loving Father God will give—and here comes the curve ball—"the Holy Spirit to those who ask him."

This sounds like regardless of what we ask for—including the return of adult offspring to the faith—what we're liable to get, instead, is "the Holy Spirit." Which is nice, we may think to ourselves, but that's not what we were asking for. What we wanted is our kids back practicing their faith and living their lives as good Catholics.

The point is that petitionary prayer, no matter what we ask for, has some theological twists and turns we need to be aware of. First, we must remember that prayer isn't magic; that is, when we ask God for anything at all, the simple fact that we ask does not guarantee that we will get what we want. Were this how petitionary prayer worked, we would have control over God, which is impossible, for there is no way the finite can control the infinite. Second, we know from plain human experience that when we ask God for something, quite often we don't get exactly what we asked for.

Ultimately, our prayer must be a prayer of surrender to God's frequently incomprehensible love. Bottom-line prayer for Christians is imitation of the prayer of Jesus in the Garden of Gethsemane: "Thy will be done." (See Matthew 6:10 and 26:42.) Our final prayer always must be an acknowledgment that our perspectives are limited; we can't see the Big Picture that our Father in heaven can see. Our final prayer always must be the request that God give to wandering offspring the kinds of healing and liberation they need the most and that God bring them home—whatever that may mean—in his own good time. Our final prayer must be a request for the grace to be for adult offspring who are alienated from the church the way God is for them—and that's a position of unconditional love and forgiveness.

The meaning of Jesus' words that God will give us the Holy Spirit if we ask is before us now. Ultimately, what we ask is to be for adult offspring estranged from the church as God is for them, and if we receive the gift of the Holy Spirit, this is what we will do, for our love for children estranged from the church will be one with God's love for them. Thus, our petitions to God to bring adult offspring back to the church is inseparable from surrender to God's mysterious will and love for them in all things. From this stance, parents praying for wandering adult children will find themselves praying with confidence and trust. As in so many other situations, here, too, parents do well to reflect on the words of Blessed Julian of Norwich (1343–1443): "All shall be well, and all shall be well, and all manner of thing shall be well."

In some cases wandering adult children will indeed return to the church and to the practice of the Catholic faith in which they were raised. In other cases they will not. Parents whose adult offspring return to the church will, of course, be thankful and express their thanks freely to God. But no life is trouble free, and these parents will continue to pray for their children. It is part of the vocation of Christian parents to keep praying for their children, no matter how old they get or where their lives take them. It's a lifelong business, praying for our children.

Parents whose adult offspring have not (yet) returned to the church need to guard against giving up. No matter how hopeless it may seem, parents do well to never stop praying for this homecoming. As they continue to love their children unconditionally, they also continue to pray for them and for their return to the church. No matter how many years go by, it is always possible for a return to happen. Hearts can be changed by prayer when nothing else makes a difference, and as long as life lasts there is always the possibility that a coming home to the church will occur.

When Marcie was forty-three years old, she found herself divorced, the mother of three twenty-something children who were on their own, and no longer as sure of herself and as sure of the meaning of it all as she once was. One day she happened to meet Clara, a friend from college she hadn't seen in years who had never married. The two women agreed to get together later in the week for lunch.

When the two women met a few days later, in the course of their conversation Clara happened to mention how she looked forward each week to the Sunday evening Mass at her parish church. Marcie explained that she had been away from the church for many years. Clara expressed sympathy and understanding, but she also invited Marcie to join her for Mass some Sunday evening. "I'll think about it," Marcie said. The two women exchanged phone numbers, and in the days that followed Marcie was surprised to find herself thinking about joining Clara for Mass. Finally she called her friend, who said that she would pick up Marcie the following Sunday evening.

Much about the liturgy was different from what Marcie remembered, but she was touched by the contemplative spirit of this quiet evening Mass and the simple chant used to sing its various parts. During Communion, Marcie remained in her place, but when Clara returned from receiving Communion she noticed as Marcie wiped tears away. Clara put her arm around Marcie and gave her a sideways hug. The two women attended Mass together each week for four weeks, and in the parish bulletin that fourth week, Marcie read a notice about the beginning of a new series of inquiry sessions for Catholics thinking about returning to the church.

To make a rather long story short, Marcie attended the sessions, liked what she heard, and a few months later received the Sacrament of Reconciliation and formally returned to the church. The clincher came, however, when she returned to her hometown, to the home of her elderly father—Marcie's mother had died several years earlier—to be with him for Christmas. When Marcie told her father that she had "come home to the church," she gazed in disbelief as tears sprang to his eyes and rolled down his cheeks. After he wiped the tears away and blew his nose, the old man said quietly, "I'm so glad, I am so happy. I've been praying for this for so many, many years. You can't imagine," he said with a smile.

One of the main difficulties parents often have with praying for adult children who have fallen away from the church is that we live in an instant gratification culture. In countless ways the dominant popular culture encourages and conditions us to expect immediate satisfaction or results. When we want something we, by golly, want it now. Manufacturers market everything from microwave ovens to headache remedies by emphasizing how quickly we can expect the product to give us what we want from it. A meal in a minute! No headache fast! When it turns out that our prayers of petition for the return of wayward grown children don't work this way, however, we tend to get discouraged and give up.

Perhaps one good way to cultivate the patience we need to keep praying—sometimes for many years—is to consider a simple fact. Look at how patient God is, and has been, with you. How many years has your Father in heaven been patient with you when it comes to ways in which you lack faith and lack trust in him? Let's face it, there are numerous ways in which most of us are just plain lazy about getting our spiritual act together and living our Catholic faith as we should. Yet God our loving Father never gives up on us, not for a second, year after year, decade after decade.

Ultimately, of course, it's possible that fallen-away offspring may never return to the practice of the Catholic faith. God created them free, and some can and will make that choice. Parents need to accept this as a possibility while realizing—as we acknowledged above, and it bears repeating—that God is bigger than the church, and his unconditional love for wayward offspring never ends. Even outside the church Christ holds adult offspring estranged from the church in his care. In the long run, prayer for grown children remains a part of the vocation of parenthood.

As parents we need to remain faithful to prayer for our grown offspring who have fallen away from the church. Otherwise, we can't say we have done all that we could, right up until the day we die. Indeed, there is nothing unique about this for parents whose kids are away from the church. As mentioned, whether our adult offspring are in or out of the church, part of the lifelong vocation of parenthood is daily prayer for our children. That's the way it is.

AFTERWORD

Why Be Catholic?

In the introduction to this book, I wrote about a young woman I met who described herself as "a very lapsed Catholic." I described our conversation and how I told her that I hoped that one day she would be able to come home to the church. From my remarks to her came the title for this book: "It's not the same without you." If this young woman ever does think about returning to the church, it wouldn't surprise me if at some point in the coming-home process she were to ask an important question: "Why should I return to the church? Why should I want to be Catholic?"

Basic to this book is the assumption that the Catholic Church is worth returning to, that those who are alienated from the church do well to come home again. In particular, this book presumes that it makes more sense for a fallen-away Catholic to return to the Catholic Church than to affiliate with another Christian church or sect, with a non-Christian religion, or to become merely indifferent toward religion. Therefore, the reader deserves something by way of a rationale for this assumption.

Also: In many, perhaps most, cases, people return to the church for deeply personal reasons intricately tied to their life experiences. Sometimes, however, so that the process is not entirely subjective, it can also help if someone presents those thinking of returning with some objective reasons for coming home to the Catholic Church.

Ironically, one of the facts that can make it more difficult to return to the church is the Catholic Church's broad-minded attitude. Indeed, the Catholic Church is the only Christian church that, by its own doctrines, is obliged to admit that God is bigger than the Catholic Church and that salvation is, in fact, available outside the church, in other churches and other religious traditions.

One of the major shifts in focus made in the mid-1960s by the Second Vatican Council was to acknowledge that saving grace, not to mention saving goodness, truth, and beauty, is present in other religions, and that the risen Christ is present and active in non-Catholic Christian communities and even outside faith communities in secular society. The Catholic

Church also insists that it is essential to respect the spiritual freedom of every person to choose his or her spiritual and religious paths in the world.[1]

At the same time, the Catholic Church, in all humility, also insists that only in the Catholic Church, despite all its imperfections and faults, does the potential exist to be in communion with the fullness of the Gospel and the fullness of the presence of the risen Christ. Only the Catholic Church can trace its existence in an uninterrupted historical line back to the earliest Christian communities, through those communities to the apostles of Jesus, and through them to Jesus himself.[2] This line is far from being without its periods of infidelity to the Gospel, to be sure, but ultimately it is always marked by self-reform and return to a more faithful observance.

The last thing I would want to suggest is that the Catholic Church is without faults. As a worldwide faith community we, the church, have our blind spots. The pope teaches infallibly under very limited circumstances, in spite of the efforts of ultraconservative Catholics to teach that the pope is virtually infallible all of the time. From the pope to parish priests and the most ordinary parish lay minister, the church's leaders are just as likely to make mistakes and leave common sense behind as anyone else. The last thing Catholics should have is a theological superiority complex.

Sometimes other Christian churches—and even other religions—outdo the Catholic Church when it comes to living the actual spirit of the Gospel. All the same, objectively speaking—for the reasons outlined above—for someone born Catholic to choose another Christian church over a Catholic church, or to choose a non-Christian religion over Catholicism, may be compared to choosing a piece of the pie rather than the whole pie. Indeed, a major characteristic of Catholicism is that anything good, true, or beautiful found anyplace else is either already present in Catholicism, or Catholicism is perfectly compatible with it.

People born in other religious or philosophical circumstances find themselves there, and that's where their roots are, so it's perfectly understandable if that's where they remain. But for someone born and raised in the Catholic Church, leaving the church can seem like an exercise in cutting off the nose to spite the face. Once again, the words of Father Andrew Greeley come to mind: "If you can find a perfect church, go ahead and join it, but as soon as you do it won't be perfect anymore."

G. K. Chesterton, the great early twentieth-century English Catholic convert, compared the Catholic Church to a deep well and all other religions and philosophies to the shallow parts of a river or lake. "I could not abandon the faith," Chesterton said, "without falling back on something more shallow than the faith. I could not cease to be a Catholic except by becoming something more narrow than a Catholic."[3]

Remember that the word "catholic" means "universal" or "all-inclusive." This is the ideal that the church that calls itself "Catholic" strives for. To repeat, then, no matter what anyone may see that is good, true, or beautiful in another religion, philosophy, or Christian tradition, that goodness, truth, and beauty is either already present in Catholicism or it is perfectly welcome in and compatible with Catholicism.

One of the best examples of this in the late twentieth century was Thomas Merton, the convert to Catholicism and Trappist monk who became a famous writer, poet, artist, and social critic. Merton had a deep admiration for Buddhism and the disciplines of Zen meditation. He learned from Buddhism, participated in dialogues with Baptists and many other religious and philosophical traditions, and incorporated Zen meditation techniques into his own spirituality. In all this, however, Merton remained a deeply committed Catholic to his dying day.[4] A few years prior to his death, Merton wrote in his personal journal: "There is nothing more important than the gift of Catholic Faith—and keeping that faith pure and clear."[5]

If there is anything that is incompatible with Catholicism, it is anything that is less than good, true, or beautiful. If Catholicism shuts the door on something, it's because it somehow fails to measure up to being good, true, or beautiful.

The official Catholic position on other Christian churches and other religions is that, in varying degrees, they often embody the saving grace, goodness, truth, and beauty of the risen Christ. But only the Catholic Church bears the potential to communicate the fullness of Christian revelation. Imperfect as it is, mistaken as it sometimes is, and sinful and insensitive as its members often are, the Catholic Church carries the potential to be the widest, deepest, and most complete path to human meaning and fulfillment in both this world and the next. In this sense, the Catholic Church is the "Mother Church" of all the other Christian churches.

Why return to the Catholic Church? G. K. Chesterton's words make as much sense today as they did when he wrote them in the 1930s: "I could not cease to be a Catholic except by becoming something more narrow than a Catholic."

To this perfectly accurate statement from the 1930s, however, add some words from our own era. In 1996 when Paul Wilkes's excellent book *The Good Enough Catholic* was published, I was happy to find that he quoted me in the epilogue when he wanted to sum up the value of being Catholic. I trust Paul Wilkes's judgment, so I'll follow his example. Here are the words he quoted, and I do think they are right on the money. Why be Catholic? Here's why: "You will find in Catholicism the greatest potential to experience God's self-gift, or grace. You will find in the Catholic Church the most reliable opportunity to discover the truth about yourself, about other people, about life, and about the world we live in."[6]

NOTES

Introduction

1. This is a curious application of the term "recovering," since it implies that Catholicism, a religion, is like an addictive substance. Of course, the term "recovering Catholic" carries an attempt at ironic humor, which is probably the point.

2. See Andrew M. Greeley, *The Catholic Myth: The Behavior and Beliefs of American Catholics* (New York: Charles Scribner's Sons, 1990), chapter 6.

3. Ibid., 115.

4. Father Greeley concludes that this 15 percent defection rate has not changed since 1960. See ibid., 111 and 115.

5. See Mitch Finley, "The Dark Side of Natural Family Planning," *America,* February 23, 1991.

6. Richard Bausch, *Good Evening Mr. & Mrs. America and All the Ships at Sea* (New York: HarperPerennial, 1997), 110.

7. Gerald O'Collins, S.J., and Edward G. Farrugia, S.J., *A Concise Dictionary of Theology,* revised edition (Mahwah, NJ: Paulist Press, 2000), 124.

Chapter 1

1. For the full story on the papal advisory commission on birth control, see Robert McClory, *Turning Point: The Inside Story of the Papal Birth Control Commission, and How* Humanae Vitae *Changed the Life of Patty Crowley and the Future of the Church* (New York: Crossroad Publishing Co., 1995).

Chapter 2

1. See Paul Wilkes, *The Good Enough Catholic: A Guide for the Perplexed* (New York: Ballantine Books, 1996).

2. This sixteenth-century position was reversed by the Second Vatican Council in the mid-1960s.

Chapter 3

1. John Henry Newman, *An Essay on the Development of Christian Doctrine* (Westminster, MD: Christian Classics, Inc., 1968), 177.

2. Ibid., 278.

Chapter 5

1. George Weigel, *The Truth of Catholicism: Ten Controversies Explored* (New York: HarperCollins Publishers, 2001), 38–30.

PART TWO
The Church Has Obligations to Alienated Catholics

1. See Sheila Garcia, "Who Are Inactive Catholics?" *The Evangelist* (Diocese of Albany, NY), July 5, 2001, 19.

2. See Father Dan Danielson, "Help Them Return." *The Evangelist* (Diocese of Albany, NY), July 5, 2001, 19.

3. Carrie Kemp, *Catholics Can Come Home Again!* (Mahwah, NJ: Paulist Press, 2001), 1.

Chapter 6

1. The quotations from Monsignor Thomas Cahalane in this section are from a document about Alienated Catholics Anonymous produced by Our Mother of Sorrows Parish, Tucson, Arizona.

2. Thomas Merton, *Thoughts in Solitude* (New York: Farrar, Straus and Giroux, 1958), 83.

3. This article is available from the Landings website: *www.landings-international.com/softplace.ssi.*

4. For the entire text of the preamble, go to: *www.landings-international.com/preamble.ssi.*

5. This article also is available from the Landings website: *www.landings-international.com/mercy.ssi.*

6. Ibid.

Chapter 7

1. For a detailed explanation and extensive quotations from church documents, see Joseph M. Champlin, *The Marginal Catholic: Challenge, Don't Crush,* revised and updated edition (Staten Island, NY: Alba House Publications, 2001), Chapter 9, "Marriage: Official Directives."

2. See for example Michael J. McManus, *Marriage Savers* (Grand Rapids, MI: Zondervan, 1993) 140ff. See also James Healy, Ph.D., *Liv-*

ing Together and Christian Commitment (1511 Jones St., Joliet, IL 60435). See also *www.rootedinlove.org.*

3. From a document written for and sent privately to the author by Father Joseph Champlin.

Chapter 8

1. Personal letter to the author.

2. From private written communication with the author.

Afterword

1. See these Vatican II documents: *Decree on Ecumenism, Declaration on the Relation of the Chruch to Non-Christian Religions,* and *Declaration on Religious Liberty.*

2. The Eastern Orthodox churches can make a similar claim, depending on one's interpretation of history, but it is outside the scope of the present discussion to get into the history of the division between the Eastern and Western churches. See Thomas Bokenkotter, *A Concise History of the Catholic Church,* revised and expanded edition (New York: Doubleday & Co., 1990). See also Clark Carlton, *The Faith: Understanding Orthodox Christianity—An Orthodox Catechism* (Salisbury, MA: Regina Orthodox Press, 1997).

3. G. K. Chesterton, *The Well and the Shallows* (London: 1935), quoted in Joseph Pearce, *Wisdom and Innocence: A Life of G.K. Chesterton* (San Francisco: Ignatius Press, 1996), p. 464.

4. See Mitch Finley, "The Joy of Being Catholic: The Relationship of the Conversion of Thomas Merton to the RCIA," in *The Merton Annual: Studies in Culture, Spirituality & Social Concerns,* Vol. 13 (Glasgow, Scotland: Sheffield Academic Press, 2000), 171–189.

5. Thomas Merton, *Dancing in the Water of Life: Seeking Peace in the Hermitage,* ed. Robert E. Daggy; Journals V, 1963–1966, (San Francisco: HarperSanFrancisco, 1997), 317.

6. Mitch Finley, *Catholic Is Wonderful! How to Make the Most of It* (Totowa, NJ: Resurrection Press, 1994) 15.

MITCH FINLEY is the author of more than thirty books on Catholic topics and the recipient of twelve Catholic Press Association Awards, the Thomas More Medal for a Distinguished Contribution to Catholic Literature, and an Excellence in Writing Award from the American Society of Journalists and Authors. He earned a Bachelor of Arts in Religious Studies from Santa Clara University and a Master of Arts in Theology from Marquette University. He has written for publications such as *Reader's Digest, Christian Science Monitor, America, National Catholic Reporter, Our Sunday Visitor,* and many more. Finley has taught theology at Gonzaga University and been a syndicated columnist for Catholic News Service. He lives with his wife, Kathy, in Spokane, Washington, where he is the events coordinator for a large independent bookstore.